# The Workers of Namibia

by

**Gillian and Suzanne Cronje**

This report is based on material prepared for the Anti-Slavery Society and submitted by them in 1977 to the Third Session of the Working Group of Experts on Slavery of the United Nations Sub-Commission on Prevention of Discrimination and Protection of Minorities.

**International Defence and Aid Fund for Southern Africa**

104 Newgate Street, London EC1A 7AP

London February 1979

The International Defence and Aid Fund for Southern Africa has the following objects:-

1. To aid, defend and rehabilitate the victims of unjust legislation and oppressive and arbitrary procedures;

2. To support their families and dependants;

3. To keep the conscience of the world alive to the issues at stake.

ISBN No. 0 904759 27 X

# Contents

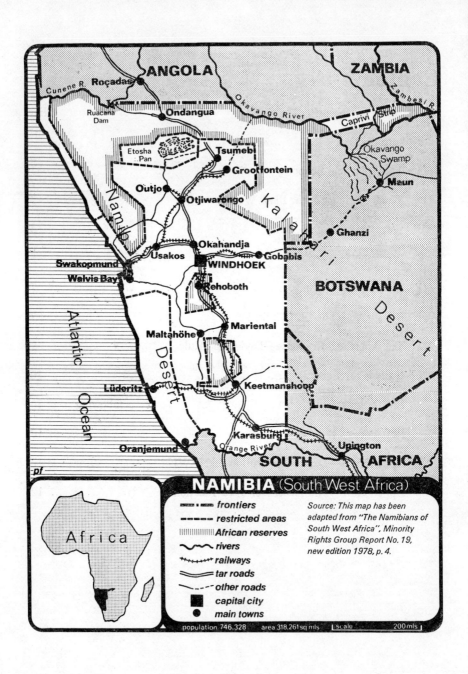

ANGOLA

ZAMBIA

Cunene R.   Roçadas

Okavango River

Zambesi R.

Ruacana Dam

Ondangua

Caprivi Strip

Etosha Pan

Tsumeb

Okavango Swamp

Grootfontein

Maun

Outjo

Kalahari

Otjiwarongo

Ghanzi

Okahandja

Swakopmund

Usakos

Gobabis

WINDHOEK

Walvis Bay

Rehoboth

BOTSWANA

Nam̃ib

Desert

Maltahöhe

Mariental

Atlantic Ocean

Desert

Lüderitz

Keetmanshoop

Karasburg

Oranjemund

Orange River

Upington

SOUTH

AFRICA

pf

## NAMIBIA (South West Africa)

|  | |
|---|---|
| ▬ ▪ ▬ | frontiers |
| ---- | restricted areas |
| ⦚⦚⦚ | African reserves |
| ∿∿ | rivers |
| ✚✚✚ | railways |
| ═ | tar roads |
| --- | other roads |
| ■ | capital city |
| ● | main towns |

Africa

Source: This map has been adapted from "The Namibians of South West Africa", Minority Rights Group Report No. 19, new edition 1978, p. 4.

population 746,328   area 318,261 sq mls   scale   200 mls

# I

# Introduction

We are dissatisfied with the fact that our mineral resources and other wealth are being exported. They are squeezing our country dry. Because it is a fact that this country is our country. We are in the majority in this country and we are the very people who are suffering, while the foreigners who have come from somewhere in our country are the ones who are giving orders and getting all the wealth of our country.

Therefore we workers feel that we have to unite so that we can take action to end the exploitation of man by man.

This statement was made by a Namibian contract worker, interviewed in Windhoek in 1977.[1] It is one of the many sources that *The Workers of Namibia* has drawn upon in compiling a picture of Namibia's black workers and their struggle against South African occupation of their country. While a number of excellent books and other material have been published on this subject, they are not always easily available to the wider reading public. Part of the purpose of this book is to fill this gap.

In recent years Namibia—one of Africa's last and most easily forgotten colonies—has come into the news. The initiatives taken by the five Western members of the United Nations Security Council to secure Namibia's independence through negotiations with the South African government have, in particular, received considerable coverage in the overseas press and media. Yet few people in the West are aware of the underlying suffering and economic hardship that have fired the Namibian people's resistance to colonial rule for over a century. For a brief moment—towards the end of 1971 and the beginning of 1972—the territory's black labour force made its mark on the world's press when more than 13,000 contract workers came out on general strike. Since then, however, the plight of Namibia's black workers and their families, and their continuing efforts to hit back at the apartheid regime, have been by and large overlooked or ignored.

In September 1974 the United Nations Council for Namibia enacted a Decree to protect the natural resources of the people of Namibia and to ban the export of the territory's raw materials without the UN's consent. The Decree was subsequently endorsed by the UN General Assembly, which requested all Member States to take appropriate action to ensure that it was put into effect.[2] Despite Namibia's status as one of the most crucial international issues of the present day, however, relatively little attention has been paid to the activities

5

of the many overseas companies which continue to invest in and trade with the territory, or to the wages and conditions of their black employees. The Parliamentary Select Committee set up by the British government in 1973 to investigate the wages paid by British companies in South Africa, for example, chose not to concern itself with Namibia.[3] The economic consequences of South Africa's illegal occupation of the territory are nevertheless of crucial significance in the international dispute over Namibia's destiny and will pose immense and pressing problems for its leadership in the future.

The history of the Namibian people's struggle against South African rule, and the aims and ideals that have inspired their national liberation movement, the South West Africa People's Organization (SWAPO), make it clear that there can be no genuine and acceptable independence for Namibia without far-reaching changes in the present patterns of economic exploitation of the black labour force.

The conditions under which the vast majority of Namibia's black workers are forced to live, and the web of restrictions and controls which binds them to their employers and prevents them from moving freely around the country, have often been described as akin to slavery. Up to two-thirds of the labour force—a higher proportion than almost anywhere else in the world, including South Africa itself—are migrants, permitted to remain in the country's white industrial and farming areas only so long as they are required by the apartheid economy. This migrant or contract labour system is crucial to South Africa's occupation of Namibia and, of all aspects of apartheid, is the one most deeply resented by black workers. It requires workers who participate in the white economy to do so on a temporary basis, returning to the tribal reserves or "homelands" at the end of their terms of service. Contract workers are unable to bring their families with them when they travel from the "homelands" to the "white" areas, and are forced to live as single men in barrack-like dormitories or hostels, while their families must manage as best they can during the prolonged absence of the chief wage-earner. The vast majority of black Namibians, whether caught up in the contract system or not, live in conditions of extreme poverty—in a country which possesses some of the richest and most abundant natural resources in Africa.

It is these resources, notably of diamonds, uranium, copper and other strategic minerals in worldwide demand, which help to explain South Africa's determination to retain control of Namibia and why, as the end of the 1970s approaches, it remains as firmly entrenched in the territory as ever before. Namibia is both a geographical and political buffer between the apartheid state and the rest of independent Africa, and a rich storehouse of the raw materials which would be crucial to South Africa's survival in the event of the enforcement of international economic sanctions. In its efforts to fend off United Nations and Western demands for Namibia's independence, South Africa is undoubtedly counting on the sympathy and support of the many overseas companies, particularly British and American outside of South Africa itself, which over the years have sought a share in the territory's riches. Namibia's economy is dominated by foreign private investment—to the extent that up to 50% of its Gross Domestic Product is estimated to be creamed off every year in the form of dividends and remittances abroad.

The history of Namibia throughout the colonial period is one of exploitation, both of the country's vast natural resources and of its human potential, which has been used by all its conquerors as the cheapest of labour. In 1915, during the First World War, South African troops acting on British orders took over what was then a German colony. Namibia had endured for 40 years a particularly brutal example of foreign occupation. The indigenous population had been forcibly dispossessed of their land and cattle, and over 80,000, including 60,000 of the Herero people, had lost their lives at the hands of the German army. South African rule, however, was destined to bring little improvement. In 1920 the League of Nations, conscious of the German colonial record of genocide and land seizure, conferred a mandate on South Africa to administer Namibia and to "promote to the utmost the material and moral well-being and the social progress of the inhabitants" of the territory.[4] Under the terms of the mandate, South Africa was not to profit from its rights of administration. But instead of repairing the damage done by the Germans, the South African authorities proceeded to systematically enforce their emerging policies of apartheid and to strip the remaining inhabitants, especially those in the north of Namibia who to date had remained relatively unscathed by colonial conquest, of their land and civil rights. As early as 1922 the South African government announced its plans for "native reserves" for the Namibian people. The foundations of the present-day pattern of racial segregation and the migrant labour system had been firmly laid. After the Second World War, when the United Nations replaced the League of Nations, South Africa refused to relinquish the mandated territory of Namibia or to concede that the UN held any jurisdiction over it.

South African attitudes to the "sacred trust" of its League of Nations mandate appeared quite early. Black Namibians existed first and foremost to serve the white-owned economy. The South West Africa* Administrator's report for 1920, for instance, declared that "the native question. . . is synonymous with the labour question".[5] Africans were tolerated in white-occupied areas "principally or solely as a labour supply for adjacent farms".[6] The South African authorities drew attention in their annual reports on the territory to improved sanitation as a means of increasing the African population and thereby the work-force; healthy black children "represent potential labourers of the future", and "the happier the native was the better he worked". Even so, employers complained of a labour shortage and it was not long before ways and means began to be sought to compel the black population to join the wage sector. Taxes, to be paid in cash, were introduced "to induce labourers to come out to work"—one group was made to pay a dog tax, for example. Africans who were "dilatory

*South Africa has always refused to recognise the United Nations' choice, in 1968, of "Namibia" as the territory's official name. The colonial name "South West Africa" is used in the text only where appropriate to refer to South African legislation and official practice.

in finding employment" were threatened with deportation from white-occupied areas under the Vagrancy Act. Alternatively, convicts were hired out to "suitable employers". The church was caught up in the system, with Christian missions being required to urge "all natives under their influence to seek employment in South West Africa". Welfare officers were sent to the African reserves "to see that there was no loafing", and it was pointed out that these areas had not been set aside to enable Africans "to lead a lazy life", but rather for "native servants out at work to place their stock . . . and to collect there the old and infirm".[7]

These statements were made in the early years of South Africa's mandate, but so consistently have the policies they mirrored been enforced that they could apply equally well to conditions today. In fact, white officials can still be heard expounding much the same kind of attitudes towards Africans as little more than labour units.

Despite the territory's legal status as an international trust, South Africa has persistently enforced its own apartheid policies in Namibia. Most of South Africa's racial and repressive laws, designed to ensure the subjection of the black population and the supremacy of the white, have been extended to Namibia just as if it were part of the Republic. Namibians are classified by their South African rulers into 12 "ethnic" or "population groups"—one "white", three "Coloured" and eight "African", "Bantu" or "native".[8] As is the case for South Africa itself, "Coloureds" and "Africans" are both generally described, and regard themselves as black. This terminology is used in this book except where, because of administrative or legislative practice, it is necessary to differentiate between African and Coloured.

South Africa has always maintained that this racial heterogencity makes a conventional democratic form of government unworkable. In place of the "unjudicious granting of independence" to the Namibian people, it has argued for the giving to "each of the respective population groups . . . its own inalienable homeland [and] unlimited possibilities of self-development and fulfilment on their own native soil"[9]—in other words, for the creation of bantustans or tribal "homelands" on the South African model. Active steps have in fact been taken to incorporate Namibia completely into the Republic of South Africa as a fifth province. While this attempt at international hijacking has been thwarted by the growing successes of the Namibian liberation struggle, South Africa has remained adamant that a portion of Namibia—the economically crucial and politically strategic port of Walvis Bay—must remain part of South Africa. The Walvis Bay enclave, which up to that time had been administered as part of Namibia, was annexed in August 1977 and declared to be part of the Cape Province.

The Namibian people have never submitted meekly to foreign occupation of their land. At the present time, South African rule is maintained through military force, and the deployment of up to 60,000 troops in the territory, not to mention the South African police. Massive military bases have been established at Grootfontein and Walvis Bay in particular, from which fighter jets can

8

be despatched as necessary to bomb strategic targets both in Namibia and neighbouring Angola.  Since February 1972, the northern part of the territory has been administered through what to all intents and purposes amounts to martial law, under which the South African police and army possess sweeping powers to suppress political activity and to harass, arrest and detain suspected supporters of SWAPO and the armed liberation struggle.  (While the emergency Proclamations R 17 and R 89, each of which had imposed severe restrictions on freedom of movement and speech in northern Namibia, were repealed in November 1977, they were immediately replaced with new and only marginally less stringent security measures, which remain fully in force).  As the guerilla fighters of the People's Liberation Army of Namibia (PLAN - SWAPO's military wing) have grown in numbers and experience, the South African army has mounted increasingly aggressive and destructive reprisals—culminating, in May 1978, in the massacre of 600 black Namibians at Cassinga refugee camp in southern Angola.

South Africa is recognised by the international community to have been in illegal occupation of Namibia for more than 12 years.  On 27 October 1966 the United Nations General Assembly overwhelmingly resolved to terminate South Africa's mandate over South West Africa, as Namibia was then called, and to make the territory a direct UN responsibility.[10]  This position was confirmed by the UN Security Council on 20 March 1969.[11]  In 1971, after a protracted wrangle, the International Court of Justice, in an Advisory Opinion, decided that the termination of the mandate by the General Assembly was legal.[12]

South Africa has reacted to the mounting pressure for Namibia's independence by promoting its own choice of "federal" or tribal government for the territory— a "solution" which would leave it in a position to exercise decisive control over political and economic developments. In September 1975, hand-picked delegates from each of Namibia's 12 "population groups" met for the first time in the Turnhalle, a converted drill-hall in Windhoek.  The Turnhalle constitutional talks, whose deliberations were universally condemned both inside Namibia and overseas, duly came up with a set of constitutional proposals which would have left the status quo in the territory substantially unchanged, with some cosmetic changes in apartheid law and practice.  The Turnhalle formula, which is essentially a modified version of South Africa's bantustan policy, has continued to form the basis of the South African government's strategy for Namibia.  While the constitutional talks were formally dissolved following the appointment by South Africa of an Administrator-General to supervise Namibia's transition to independence, the participants were resuscitated in the form of a tribally-based political party, the Democratic Turnhalle Alliance (DTA).  It was clear from early in 1978 that the DTA was destined to receive massive official backing and would be the South African government's choice to win any elections organised in Namibia prior to independence.

On 20 September 1978, in his last public act before retiring from office, South Africa's Prime Minister Vorster finally set the seal of failure on a year

9

and a half of diplomatic manoeuvrings by the five Western members of the UN Security Council to achieve a negotiated settlement of the Namibian issue. He announced the South African government's rejection of proposals formulated by the United Nations Secretary-General for Namibia's transition to independence, and its intention to press ahead unilaterally with elections in the territory without further delay. In a statement delivered in Zambia by its Vice-President, SWAPO made it clear that in the view of the Namibian liberation movement, South Africa had now closed "all doors to a peaceful settlement of the Namibian question and have instead chosen the war path".[13]

Namibia's black workers, as is shown in more detail in this book, have always formed the backbone of Namibia's liberation movement. There is no doubt that resistance in the work place will continue to form an integral part of the Namibian people's wider struggle for their country's freedom and independence.

Chapters II to VI below describe the conditions under which Namibia's black labour force live and work, the implications of the apartheid economy, and particularly the contract labour-system, for family life, and the suppression of trade union organizations and strike action. Chapters VII to IX document the history of workers' resistance to South African rule, the origins of SWAPO within the contract system, and the attempts of the apartheid authorities to exploit "tribal" sentiments to split and weaken the liberation movement.

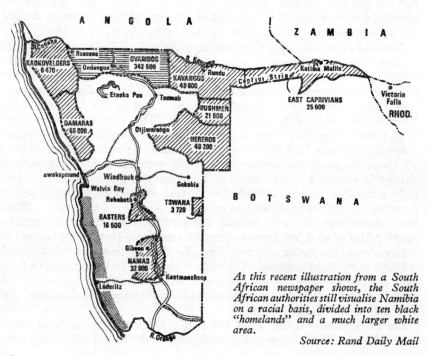

*As this recent illustration from a South African newspaper shows, the South African authorities still visualise Namibia on a racial basis, divided into ten black "homelands" and a much larger white area.*

*Source: Rand Daily Mail*

**Table I    Namibia's Population: South Africa's Suspect Figures**

| Population group | Number | | Percentage of total population | | Percentage of each group living in their "homeland" |
|---|---|---|---|---|---|
| | 1970 | 1974 | 1970 | 1974 | 1970 |
| Ovambos | 352,640 | 396,000 | 46,3 | 46,5 | 83% |
| Whites | 90,583 | 99,000 | 11,9 | 11,6 | —— |
| Damaras | 66,291 | 75,000 | 8,7 | 8,8 | 12% |
| Hereros | 50,589 | 56,000 | 6,6 | 6,6 | 58% |
| Kavangos | 49,512 | 56,000 | 6,5 | 6,6 | 96% |
| Namas | 32,935 | 37,000 | 4,3 | 4,3 | —— |
| Coloureds | 28,512 | 32,000 | 3,7 | 3,8 | —— |
| East Caprivians | 25,580 | 29,000 | 3,3 | 3,4 | 98% |
| Bushmen | 22,830 | 26,000 | 3,0 | 3,0 | 30% |
| Rehoboth Basters | 16,649 | 19,000 | 2,2 | 2,2 | —— |
| Kaokolanders | 6,567 | 7,000 | 0,9 | 0,8 | 96% |
| Tswanas | 4,407 | 5,000 | 0,6 | 0,6 | 19% |
| Other | 15,089 | 15,000 | 2,0 | 1,8 | —— |
| Total | 762,184 | 852,000 | 100,0 | 100,0 | —— |

*Sources and notes:* The population figures for 1970 and 1974 are taken from the *South West Africa Survey* 1974, published by the South African Department of Foreign Affairs. Those for 1970 are derived from the South African government's Population Census of 6 May 1970 and those for 1974 are official estimates.

The figures showing the percentage of each "population group" living in its respective "homeland" are derived from information in *Homelands—the Role of the Corporations*, a promotional publication for the South African Bantu Investment Corporation, Chris van Rensburg Publications (Pty) Ltd., p. 33.

South Africa has revised its population statistics for Namibia several times in recent years, in the light of international concern over the territory. In October 1975, for example, the Afrikaans national newspaper *Die Suidwes-Afrikaner* published figures attributed to official sources. These showed a total population of 917,100, of whom 86,4% were black, 11,7% white and 1,9% 'others' (*Zimbabwe-Namibia, Anticipation of Economic and Humanitarian Needs*, African-American Scholars Council 1977, Appendix II).

All South African population figures are suspect. The smaller the population of Namibia, the less obvious it becomes how little South Africa is spending per head on social services, education, etc, and also the less important the Namibian problem can be made to appear in international eyes.

The population of Namibia in 1977 has been estimated by an independent researcher as between 950, and 1,010,000, of which 850-900,000 are blacks and 100-110,000 are whites (W. H. Thomas, *Economic Development in Namibia — Towards Acceptable Development Strategies for Independent Namibia*, Kaiser-Grünewald 1978 p. 19)

A study prepared for the United Nations Namibia Institute in Lusaka, however, has concluded that Namibia's population is probably of the order of 1,250,000, made up of slightly over 100,000 Europeans (excluding South African military personnel who would raise the total to 150,000), 115,000 Coloureds and 1,035,000 Africans. (*Towards Manpower Development for Namibia — Background Notes*, by Prof. R. H. Green, United Nations Institute for Namibia 1978).

# II

# The Apartheid Economy

Namibia possesses a rich variety of natural resources, notably minerals and precious stones. It is potentially one of the wealthiest countries in Africa, yet the economic policies that have been pursued during the years of South African occupation—and indeed before—have contrived to leave the vast majority of its people in a state of extreme poverty. South Africa, for its part, has endeavoured to disguise the fact that it has gained enormous financial advantages from the territory.

As in the Republic itself, the South African authorities have consistently enforced the apartheid policy of bantustans or "homelands" in Namibia. The population has been classified on a racial basis into 12 "ethnic" or "population groups" each of which, with the exception of "whites" and "Coloureds", has been allocated its own, ultimately "self-governing", "homeland" or tribal reserve. About 40% of the territory has been designated in this way for the black population and 43% for the use of the whites, with the remainder, including all the main diamond-bearing areas of Namibia, coming directly under South African government control. Partition has been carried out in such a way that all the country's main mining and manufacturing enterprises are situated in the "white" area, as is all the most productive arable and stock rearing land, while the "homelands" are, in the main, impoverished backwaters turned over to subsistence agriculture. Their major contribution to the white-owned economy is as a pool of cheap and plentiful unskilled labour.

Because the "homelands" or reserves are incapable of supporting their populations, the vast majority of black Namibians face the choice of working for wages for a white employer, or starvation. Additional measures, such as taxation, have been employed by the authorities to force black workers to leave the reserves to seek employment in the white zone as migrant labourers. The story of black workers in Namibia is first and foremost the story of the contract labour system; between half and threequarters of the black labour force is made up of migrant workers—one of the highest proportions in the world. Apart from a minority who have acquired rights of permanent residence in black townships or farms in the white zone, black workers are not permitted to have their families with them and must return to the reserves at the termination of their labour contracts. They have minimal rights in the white areas and are obliged to live in regimented "single men's" hostels or compounds, frequently over-crowded and subject to constant supervision by employers and police.

This system, developed and enforced over many years of colonial rule,

13

dominates the experience of black Namibians today. While from time to time the South African authorities have permitted minor modifications—in particular, and most recently, the abolition of certain aspects of the "pass laws" or influx control—the essentials remain firmly entrenched.

## Economic Structure

Building up a picture of the Namibian economy is by no means a straightforward matter. Much of the requisite statistical and other information has been withheld by the South African authorities since the early 1960s, or disguised by being aggregated with figures for the Republic of South Africa itself. Such figures as are released are carefully selected to give the impression, as one commentator has put it, that Namibia is an "economically unviable territory heavily dependent on South African subsidisation and unable to sustain the economic burden of independence,"[1] or to put it another way, that South Africa's occupation of the territory has been a kind of vast philanthropic exercise, motivated solely by concern for the welfare of its inhabitants. In fact, those sectors of the economy which have received the greatest input of skills and capital resources have been those which bring the greatest rewards for South African and overseas investors.

One of the most striking things about Namibia is its mineral wealth—diamonds, lead, tin, uranium, zinc and copper. The economy of the country today is dominated by the mining industry, which in turn is largely controlled by overseas multinational companies. It has been estimated that during the early 1970s investment was flowing into Namibia at the rate of around £25 million a year—and that 60% of this was going into mining.[2] The mining boom, which started after World War II, today contributes well over half of the value of Namibia's exports (it has been estimated that the figure may have risen to 71.5% in 1977[3]—see also Table III p. 17), while one-third of the country is covered by mining concessions or temporary prospecting permits.[4] All the major companies are foreign owned, the most important being Consolidated Diamond Mines, a subsidiary of the giant Anglo-American Corporation of South Africa which holds a monopoly over diamond mining in Namibia; the Tsumeb Corporation, mining copper, lead and zinc, together with smaller quantities of cadmium and silver, and controlled by United States interests, (American Metal Climax (AMAX) and the Newmont Mining Corporation); and Rössing Uranium Ltd., operating the largest open cast uranium mine in the world, near Swakopmund, and 60% owned by the Rio Tinto-Zinc Corporation (RTZ) of Great Britain. (Uranium has begun to figure in the Namibian economy relatively recently, while diamonds have been exploited for many years, accounting for around two thirds of all the territory's mineral sales. Namibia is in fact the largest producer of gem diamonds in the world. A number of other multinational companies have recently been prospecting for uranium—discoveries which could only increase the international contest over the territory.)

The two other most important economic sectors, in terms of their contribution to Gross Domestic Product (GDP), are factory fishing, based at the ports of

Walvis Bay and Luderitz, and commercial stock raising particularly of karakul sheep (*see Table II p.* 16). Namibia produces about half the world's supply of luxury karakul (persian lamb) pelts. Like mining, both these industries are dominated by overseas multinationals. A survey undertaken in September 1973 into foreign companies investing in Namibia identified 88 such multinationals, of which 35 were South African; 25 were controlled by United Kingdom interests; 15 by United States interests; West Germany 8; France 3 and Canada 2.[5] The South African government has actively encouraged foreign investors to put their money into Namibia, particularly in recent years, with the result that a very large percentage of the territory's economic production is repatriated in the form of profits earned by overseas companies, dividends for their shareholders and wages for their expatriate employees. A comparison between Namibia's Gross Domestic Product (ie. the total value of goods and services produced in the territory) and Gross National Product (the total value after foreign payments) is a graphic illustration of this process. It has been estimated that over one third, and perhaps as much as one half of Namibia's GDP is "creamed off" each year, and that the resulting discrepancy between GDP and GNP has got gradually wider.[6] It is difficult to reach an exact figure in the absence of statistical information. As one researcher has pointed out, details "such as the annual Gross *National* Product are not disclosed to those outside the ruling groups. . . . Comparing Namibia and South Africa, the gap between GNP and GDP is thought to be one third of GNP in Namibia (but only 3.9% in South Africa). This means that a major share of the Namibian national income accrues outside the territory, to foreign interests who would clearly not favour publication of the GNP figure."[7]

Investing in Namibia has been extremely profitable for many of the companies concerned. From 1970 to 1973, for example, Consolidated Diamond Mines' (CDM) net profits rose consistently from R33.8 million to R96.5 million per annum.* In 1974 there was a drop to R80.6 million, of which R30.2 million were paid out in dividends to its (predominantly overseas) shareholders.[8] In 1970 CDM's profits constituted 44% of the total net profits of its immediate parent, De Beers Consolidated Mines, while in 1974, despite the dip in earnings, they contributed 40%.

Consolidated Diamond Mines has acquired a reputation over the years of paying the best wages available to black workers in Namibia. Yet in 1976, CDM spent only about a tenth of its net profits on wages for its black miners.[9] Wages paid to black workers in Namibia are even lower than those in South Africa, where 30 to 40% of the total product of the mining industry is paid in remuneration. The comparable figure for Namibia is 15 to 25%.[10]

The commodities boom of the early 1970s meant particularly high profits for mining companies in Namibia, a fact that did not go unnoticed by foreign investors. As the financial pages of one British newspaper put it: "South West Africa is looking a more appetizing morsel all the time".[11]

---

* One South African rand (R) is worth about £0.60p.

15

**Table II    Namibia's Economy: Contribution of Economic Sectors to Gross Domestic Product (GDP)**

| | Percentage contribution to GDP | | | |
| --- | --- | --- | --- | --- |
| | 1960 | 1965 | 1970 | 1977 |
| Agriculture, forestry and fishing | 14,9 | 15,3 | 16,0 | *18,5* |
| Mining | 33,8 | 39,1 | 30,3 | *32,2* |
| Secondary sector | 13,0 | 13,3 | 14,4 | *14,1* |
| Tertiary sector | 38,3 | 32,3 | 39,3 | *35,2* |
| | 100,0 | 100,0 | 100,0 | 100,0 |

*Sources and notes:* The figures for 1960, 1965 and 1970 are taken from W. H. Thomas: *Economic Development in Namibia — Towards Acceptable Development Strategies for Independent Namibia*, Kaiser-Grünewald 1978, Table E, p. 309. They are based on official South African statistics.

The figures for 1977 are taken from *Towards Manpower Development for Namibia — Background Notes*, United Nations Institute for Namibia, 1978, Tables 12 and 13.

As with other aspects of the Namibian economy, there is considerable difference of opinion as to how the territory's GDP should be broken down. Other United Nations Sources, for example, have concluded that mining and quarrying account for as much as 50 to 60% of Namibia's GDP. (UN Decolonization Committee Report 15 September 1977, Ch. IV, *Activities of Foreign Economic and other interests*, Annex II p. 4): W. H. Thomas, by contrast, has estimated that in 1975, mining's contribution to GDP declined to 27% (*op. cit.*).

(The difficulties in obtaining accurate statistical data on the economy are such that for the year 1976, for example, there are at least four separate estimates of Namibia's GDP; an official South African government figure of R742,6 million; two independent estimates of R755 and R826,4 million; and a United Nations estimate of R950 million. (*Namibia's Economy: The Options*, Africa Bureau Fact Sheet No. 55, May/June 1978).

The 1977 GDP has been estimated by UN sources to lie in the range R1,100 — R1,150 million. This works out at approximately R900 per inhabitant of Namibia, which is about the world average—significantly above the African average with the exception of South Africa and Zimbabwe (Rhodesia). In other words, as will be pointed out in the text (p. 43), Namibia is a rich country, whose wealth and resources are grossly unfairly distributed. (*Towards Manpower Development for Namibia, op. cit.*, p. 13)

**Table III  Namibia's Economy: Exports by Value**

| | Value in Rand (million) | | | |
|---|---|---|---|---|
| | 1976 | 1970 | 1973 (%) | 1977 (%) |
| Karakul pelts | 15,4 | 20,1 | 32,0 (10,3) | *62,5 (9,5)* |
| Livestock | 16,6 | 29,0 | 40,0 (12,9) | *67,5 (10,3)* |
| Fish products | 48,9 | 33,0 | 65,0 (21,0) | *65,0 (9,9)* |
| Diamonds | 85,0 | 75,0 | 127,0 (41,0) | *237,5 (36,3)* |
| Lead, zinc and copper concentrates | 40,4 | 39,0 | 40,0 (12,9) | *130,0 (19,8)* |
| Uranium | — | — | — | *92,5 (14,1)* |
| Other exports | 3,5 | 3,9 | 6,0 (1,9) | — |
| Total | 209,8 | 200,0 | 310,0 (100 ) | 655 (100) |

*Sources and notes:* The figures for 1966, 1970 and 1973 are taken from *Zimbabwe —Namibia: Anticipation of Economic and Humanitarian Needs,* Final Report of the African-American Scholars Council, 15 March 1977, Table 3 p. 177. They relate only to trade outside the South African Customs Union (Namibia, South Africa, Botswana, Lesotho, Swaziland).

The figures for 1977 are taken from *Towards Manpower Development for Namibia — Background Notes.* United Nations Institute for Namibia, 1978, Table 15—averages have been taken where appropriate, The uranium exports represent the first products of the Rössing mine outside Swakopmund, in which the British company Rio Tinto—Zinc Corporation has the major stake. They mean that the mining industry is now contributing over 70% of the total value of exports. The fishing industry, based on Walvis Bay, has experienced a serious decline in recent years due to over-exploitation.

Over half of Namibia's Gross Domestic Product—up to 90% for physical goods as opposed to services—is produced for export—a further illustration of the way in which foreign multinational companies, individuals and states, dominate the territory's economy. (*Towards Manpower Development for Namibia — Background Notes, op. cit., p.* 1).

The South African government, for its part, receives an important contribution to its revenue in the form of taxes and royalties paid by overseas firms operating in Namibia, particularly the mining companies. Researchers have pointed out, however, that these cash flows are not credited to Namibia in official South African accounts, and that this is one of the budgetary sleights of hand used by the authorities to claim that the territory is heavily dependent on subsidies from the public sector. In reality, once distortions of this kind have been corrected, it has been shown that Namibia provides a net cash flow to South Africa, rather than the other way around.[12]

It is estimated that about half of all Namibia's exports go to South Africa, thereby saving the Republic valuable foreign exchange at the same time as furnishing it with vital raw materials. Other exports from Namibia (for example to the United Kingdom, which accounts for an estimated 25% of Namibia's exports[13]) earn trade receipts for the South African government. In the reverse direction, South Africa has traditionally maintained Namibia as a market for its own exports, particularly of manufactured goods. About 90% of all Namibia's imports originate in South Africa,[14] while its own manufacturing and industrial sectors are weak and underdeveloped. The main manufacturing activity is the processing of food and other perishable products—in 1973, 100 out of 217 listed manufacturing and construction concerns were found to be involved in processing agricultural, silvicultural and marine raw products.[15]

Other industrial activity involves the finishing and assembling of materials imported from South Africa, together with the production of a few mineral concentrates, copper and lead smelting. (The proportion of total product paid out in the form of remuneration to employees in the manufacturing sector is, as in the mining industry, considerably lower in Namibia than in South Africa. The figures have been estimated at 30-35% and 60% respectively[16]).

### Ethnic fragmentation and the "homelands"

Namibia's economy has grown in an unbalanced and lop-sided way under South Africa's control. Resources have been concentrated in the mining industry, while much of the agricultural sector, notably the subsistence farming of the reserves, has remained backward and neglected. Namibia today, despite its sparse population, is very far from being self-sufficient in food production—a fact which can be directly attributed to South Africa's "homelands" policy.

Namibia's "homelands" are based on a blueprint drawn up in 1962-3 and published the following year, by a *Commission of Enquiry into South West African Affairs*, appointed by the South African government and headed by Mr. F. H. Odendaal. The Odendaal Report classified Namibia's population into 12 "population groups"—whites, Coloureds, Rehoboth Basters, Namas, Damaras, Hereros, Kaokovelders, Ovambos, Kavangos, Caprivians, Tswana and Bushmen—and recommended that each of the 10 black groups, with the exception of the Coloureds, should be allocated separate and ultimately "self-governing" reserves. (*See Map p.* 10).

18

The Odendaal Plan marked the acceleration of a systematic programme, begun half a century earlier, of removing the black population from the best farming land and mineral rich areas of Namibia and confining them to peripheral areas, mainly in the northern half of the country and on the desert margin. Namibia has been divided since German times into the "Police Zone", or rich southern part of the country in which the early settlers made their homes, dispossessing the indigenous African populations from their traditional grazing lands, and the "native reserves" of the north. (*See map on p.* 10). While the original concept of the "Police Zone" has since been superseded by new laws and practices, it still has relevance for the apartheid system. From the earliest days of white colonization Africans were not allowed to move outside the reserves without permits, which were generally issued only to those seeking employment in the white economy. The Odendaal Plan built upon this long-standing division of the country. Those "homelands" situated to the north of the Police Zone, notably Ovamboland and Kavangoland, provide the white economy with the bulk of its contract labour.

In the south the situation is somewhat different, as despite Namibia's long history of forced removals, most of the supposed "citizens" of those homelands located within the Police Zone live outside the areas reserved for them. Official figures reveal that 88% of all Damaras—the third largest "population group"—live outside Damaraland, 81% of Tswanas live outside the Tswana reserve and around two-fifths of the Hereros live outside Hereroland (*see Table I, p.* 11). This "absenteeism" is of course connected with the fact that the Africans have been allocated the poorest ground, which was in many cases not their traditional land, and to the lack of economic opportunity in these areas.

Following the publication of the Odendaal Report, the South African government took steps to put it into practice. In 1968, in particular, the *Development of Self-Government for Native Nations in South West Africa Act* provided for the creation of "homelands" for the Ovambos, Damaras, Hereros, Kaokolanders, Kavangos and East Caprivians. In February 1973 amendments were made to the Native Nations Act empowering the State President to grant "self-government" to a Namibian "homeland" without recourse to parliament, and Ovamboland and Kavangoland were subsequently elevated to "self-governing" status under their own "legislative councils". Despite the South African government's frequently repeated claim that the Namibian people are free to decide upon their own choice of independence constitution and that "all options are open", the racial classification on which the "homelands" are based has formed the basis for all its proposals for a constitutional settlement. In particular, the appointment in 1977 of a supposedly neutral Administrator General to supervise Namibia's transition to independence did not lead to any attempt to abandon the homelands structure or to dismantle the institutions of "self-government" that had already been set up.[17]

Even the Odendaal Report made it clear that the "homelands" were to be situated in the most arid and unproductive parts of the country. The reserves designated by the Report contained only about 500 of the 3,500 boreholes in Namibia, for example.[18] Official South African publications invariably point out that Ovamboland and Kavangoland, the two most important northern homelands, are the wettest areas of Namibia—what they do not say is that the water is unevenly distributed and that according to some calculations as much as 50% of Ovamboland, in particular, is without water altogether.[19] Almost all the population in Ovamboland is in fact concentrated around the flood plains.[20]

A number of "homelands" are situated within the Police Zone (*see Map, p.* 10). Of these, only the Rehoboth Basters could be said to occupy land comparable in quality to that owned by whites—but their population density and hence pressure on the land, is much greater. Over the country as a whole rural whites enjoy an average of 2,008 hectares per capita, while Africans in the reserves have been allocated 68 hectares per capita, and the total black population only 50 hectares per capita.[21]

Lack of natural resources, coupled with years of official neglect, means that the subsistence agriculture practised in the homelands makes practically no contribution to Namibia's GDP—in 1953, the last year for which the South African authorities provided such information, the figure was less than 3%. Observers have concluded that this situation, far from having improved, may since have deteriorated.[22] The South African authorities have deliberately discouraged the development of alternative sources of livelihood within the "homelands". Cash crop farming falls into this category, while the extensive grazing of cattle for export has been strictly controlled, for example via foot-and-mouth and other disease regulations. Residents of Ovamboland and Kavangoland "had to resort to subsistence farming rather than cash farming by constraint rather than by choice. The white-controlled SWANLA stores were not enthusiastic about purchasing crops or cattle".[23]

There are virtually no other employment opportunities in the "homelands". A few thousand Africans support themselves and their families as traders or storekeepers—they form the core of a small class of businessmen and entrepreneurs, the emergence of which has been encouraged by the South African authorities through the Bantu Investment Corporation (now renamed the Economic Investment Corporation). This government-sponsored organization was set up in 1964 following the publication of the Odendaal Report and thereupon drew up an economic development programme "with the object of creating 5,000 employment opportunities for the indigenous population during the period 1972/3 to 1976/7, entailing a capital investment of R22.5 million".[24])

Many of the jobs created by the Bantu Investment Corporation (BIC) cannot be said to have contributed to the economic development of the homeland populations as a whole as they are concentrated in retailing, in the homelands, goods manufactured by white-owned enterprises in the industrial areas—goods for which the purchasers obviously require cash and which are thereby calculated to make them increasingly dependent on the cash earnings of migratory labour. During 1971/72, African resentment against the BIC was expressed through the demands of contract workers who came out on countrywide strike—among others, that "the government must allow many types of business enterprises other than the infamous BIC which is exploiting our people".[25] Soon after the end of the strike the BIC's headquarters in Namibia, which had been in Ovamboland, were reported to have been transferred to Windhoek.[26] Despite this groundswell of resentment, the South African government went on to set up "homeland" development corporations in both Ovamboland and Kavangoland in May 1976, in terms of the *Promotion of the Economic Development of Bantu Homelands Act* of 1968, a piece of legislation designed primarily for use in South Africa, but also applied in Namibia.

A limited number of jobs are available locally in the homelands through other government agencies. Ms. Ruaha Voipio, a Finnish missionary in Ovamboland for many years, has noted however that "unemployment is also increased by the fact that contractors from the Republic bring their own teams of workers with them—even those contractors who are at work on the large development projects in the homelands. Since the Ovambos and Kavangos possess technical talents, they would have been in a position to do a great deal of the work themselves after some weeks of training, and thus new labour opportunities would have opened up in the homelands. There is bitterness because foreigners work the machines and Ovambos are only given picks and shovels."[27]

In the mineral-rich areas of the southern part of Namibia, even where mines have been established in the reserves they "have proved of little benefit to the local communities. They continue to employ migrant labour, mainly from Ovamboland, and provide no training facilities or financial contribution of any size to the 'homelands' tribal or communal authorities."[28] The state retains exclusive rights of ownership and exploitation over all minerals, precious stones, oil or other natural resources discovered in the tribal reserves, so that such finds bring little or no economic advantage to the indigenous black population.

**The black labour force**

It is self-evident from the conditions prevailing in the "homelands" that migrant labour has been forced on to black Namibians by economic necessity and oppressive legislation and not, as South African spokesmen have sometimes claimed, to earn extra money for luxuries. Virtually the whole of the black population is dependent on the wage earnings of at least one member of the family for the bare essentials of life although, in the case of contract workers, such employment is of an intermittent nature.

For various reasons, not least being the reluctance of the South African authorities to release complete statistics, it is difficult to be precise about the size and composition of the black labour force. In 1966, the last year for which the South African government published complete data on African employment, official statistics revealed a total of 69,556 male Africans employed by whites in Namibia, of whom 23,073 were employed in agriculture, 27,679 in mining, commerce and industry, 13,612 in the public sector, 3,679 in domestic service

21

and 1,513 as shopkeepers or casual labourers.[29] For subsequent years, the South African Department of Labour has published a biennial *Manpower Survey* which up to 1975 included information on Namibia as well as South Africa. These surveys are conducted on a sample basis and only cover a section of the total workforce—persons employed as domestics in private service or engaged in agriculture as wage labourers on white-owned farms are excluded completely. These two sectors of the economy, however, account for over half of all black Namibians in paid employment. In 1975 therefore, the *Manpower Survey* recorded a total of only 68,397 black Namibians, both men and women, employed in the white economy.[30] (*see Tables IV + V p.* 23 & 24.)

Professor Wolfgang Thomas, a former Director of the Institute for Social Development at the University of the Western Cape in South Africa, has estimated that in 1977, the total black labour force amounted to 272,000 men and women of whom 91,000 were engaged in subsistence agriculture and 44,000 in modern (i.e. largely white-owned) farming.[31] Professor Thomas was appointed by the South African government to a Committee of Financial Experts to advise the Turnhalle constitutional talks in Namibia. In March 1977, however, he was deported from South Africa.

A recent study of Namibia's manpower commissioned by the United Nations has produced an even higher estimate of the black labour force. Out of a total of 241,500 black workers in 1977, 50,000 were estimated to be employed on white-owned farms and ranches, and 75,000 as domestic servants. In addition, 240,000 black people were estimated to be engaged in subsistence or non-white owned agriculture, bringing the total black labour force to 481,000 (*see table IV, p.* 23).

The Namibian labour force is divided along racial lines by the official policies of apartheid, into white workers, enjoying all the privileges and freedoms associated with industrial democracy, Coloureds, occupying an intermediate position in terms of access to skills, opportunities and industrial rights, and Africans, variously described by the apartheid authorities as "Bantu" or "natives".

Within the black labour force a minority of workers (including for example the Coloureds and also many of those such as Damaras and Hereros, whose "homelands" are situated within the Police Zone) have qualified for permanent residence in the black townships of urban areas within the Police Zone, or on white-owned farms. Black workers living full-time in the white-owned parts of Namibia in this way are still subject to severe control and restrictions, particularly in respect of freedom of movement and job-seeking. Their status is always shaky; up until recently blacks were forbidden to own land anywhere in white areas and continue to face an ever-present threat of eviction and "repatriation" to the reserves.[32]

The majority of black workers in Namibia however, are migrants, subject to even more repressive legislation. Those from the northern reserves i.e. Ovamboland and Kavangoland, are employed on full-length contracts of up to 30 months at a stretch, while those originating from reserves within the Police Zone are known as "short terms" and fulfil contracts of, normally, six to 12 months.

**Table IV   Namibia's Economy: Employment Structure by Economic Sectors — 1977**

| | Number of workers | | |
| --- | --- | --- | --- |
| | White (%) | Black (%) | Total (%) |
| *Primary sector* | | | |
| White-owned agric. | 6,500 (17,8) | 50,000 (20,7) | 56,500 (20,3) |
| Fishing | 500 ( 1,4) | 7,000 ( 2,9) | 7,500 ( 2,7) |
| Mining & quarrying | 3,500 ( 9,6) | 19,000 ( 7,9) | 22,500 ( 8,1) |
| *Secondary sector* | | | |
| Manufacturing, electr. and water | 2,750 ( 7,5) | 10,250 ( 4,2) | 13,000 ( 4,7) |
| Construction | 1,750 ( 4,8) | 13,250 ( 5,5) | 15,000 ( 5,4) |
| *Tertiary sector* | | | |
| Transport & communic. | 1,000 ( 2,7) | 11,500 ( 4,8) | 12,500 ( 4,5) |
| Commerce & finance | 5,000 (13,7) | 20,000 ( 8,3) | 25,000 ( 9,0) |
| Government & other | 15,500 (42,5) | 18,000 ( 7,5) | 33,500 (12,1) |
| Domestic service | — | 75,000 (31,1) | 75,000 (27,0) |
| Unemployed | — | 17,500 ( 7,2) | 17,500 ( 6,3) |
| Total labour force | 36,500 (100 ) | 241,500 (100 ) | 278,000 (100 ) |

*Sources and notes:* The figures are derived from estimates in *Towards Manpower Development for Namibia—Background Notes.* United Nations Institute for Namibia, 1978, Table 4).

An estimated 240,000 black people employed in non-white-owned or subsistence agriculture have been excluded from the table.

The 20,000 black people employed in commerce and finance include small shopkeepers and traders.

Previous estimates of the number of black domestic servants have been much lower. e.g. Prof. W. H. Thomas includes an estimate of only 8,000 black people employed in domestic service in 1975. (W. H. Thomas, *Economic Development in Namibia — Towards Acceptable Development Strategies in Independent Namibia,* Kaiser-Grünewald 1978, Table F, p. 310).

**Table V Namibia's Manpower Structure 1969 - 1975 — South Africa's View**

|  | 1969 White | 1969 Black | 1973 White | 1973 Black | 1975 White | 1975 Black |
|---|---|---|---|---|---|---|
| A. GENERAL | 18,936 | 20,032 | 24,968 | 35,635 | 24,998 | 39,055 |
| 1 Professional, semi-professional technical | 3,266 | 1,341 | 5,447 | 3,930 | 5,877 | 5,305 |
|   Teachers | — | — | — | — | (1,500) | (3,700) |
|   Nurses | — | — | — | — | (800) | (1,600) |
| 2 Managerial, executive administrative | 1,379 | 14 | 2,180 | 37 | 2,164 | 16 |
| 3 Clerical | 5,680 | 594 | 7,248 | 1,223 | 6,483 | 1,320 |
| 4 Sales and related work | 1,732 | 938 | 2,103 | 1,896 | 2,184 | 1,955 |
| 5 Mine activities | 521 | 3,041 | 1,079 | 6,321 | 877 | 6,788 |
| 6 Transportation, delivery, communication | 1,652 | 2,223 | 1,632 | 2,715 | 1,824 | 3,317 |
| 7 Processing of metals, plastics, operatives in motor industry | 342 | 1,127 | 372 | 1,193 | 521 | 1,751 |
| 8 Operatives and semi-skilled in construction | 902 | 1,292 | 876 | 4,034 | 1,051 | 3,283 |
| 9 Processing of wood | 33 | 223 | 10 | 163 | 20 | 301 |
| 10 Washing, dry-cleaning | 24 | 178 | 43 | 323 | 16 | 294 |
| 11 Food, drink, canning, abattoirs | 216 | 3,455 | 156 | 2,900 | 241 | 2,831 |
| 12 Leather, shoe processing | 2 | 52 | 2 | 35 | 1 | 4 |
| 13 Bricks, tiles | 5 | 134 | 2 | 119 | 7 | 329 |
| 14 Chemical products | 7 | 40 | 13 | 106 | 10 | 77 |
| 15 Printing | 21 | 64 | 12 | 82 | 2 | 108 |

**Table V cont.**

|  | 1969 White | 1969 Black | 1973 White | 1973 Black | 1975 White | 1975 Black |
|---|---|---|---|---|---|---|
| 16 Supervisors and other skilled, semi-skilled | 1,479 | 1,458 | 1,829 | 4,405 | 1,830 | 5,171 |
| 17 Public, personal, and domestic services | 1,715 | 3,857 | 2,032 | 6,085 | 1,890 | 6,205 |
| B. ARTISANS, APPRENTICES | 3,426 | 1,605 | 3,964 | 1,862 | 3,563 | 2,434 |
| 19 Metal and engineering trades | 1,048 | 103 | 1,213 | 71 | — | — |
| 20 Electrical trades | 413 | 13 | 528 | 43 | — | — |
| 21 Motor trades | 821 | 54 | 1,018 | 106 | — | — |
| 22 Building trades | 851 | 1,412 | 911 | 1,588 | — | — |
| 23 27 Others | 293 | 23 | 294 | 54 | — | — |
| C. LABOURERS | 122 | 25,838 | 101 | 22,127 | 74 | 26,908 |
| SURVEY TOTAL | 22,484 | 47,475 | 29,033 | 59,624 | 28,635 | 68,397 |

*Notes* The table excludes workers employed as domestics in private service and persons engaged in subsistence agriculture and the modern farming sector —i.e. the majority of black workers.

*Source* Republic of South Africa Department of Labour Manpower Surveys 1969, 1973 and 1975, reproduced in W. H. Thomas, *Economic Development in Namibia — Towards Acceptable Development Strategies for Independent Namibia* (Kaiser Grünewald 1978, p. 169).

The 1977 Manpower Survey produced by the Department of Labour includes information for South Africa only.

The legal restrictions imposed on the latter are only marginally less harsh, as these comments from black workers interviewed in Windhoek in 1977 illustrate: Actually, there is no difference between the 'contracts' and 'short-term'— they have all come on contract. They have signed a contract between the company and the places where they come from. Let us say Metal Box went to Ovambo and it took a contract worker, and he comes to Metal Box. If he finds their conditions unsatisfactory, he cannot go and look for another job. Then he must straight away be deported to Ovambo. But a 'short-term' if he thinks that the conditions are not good for him, he has still got another chance of looking for another job.[33]

Contract workers have been variously estimated to constitute between half and threequarters of all black employees in Namibia. Here again, statistics are difficult if not impossible to come by and may deal exclusively with Ovambo contract workers, the largest group. Official South African figures for 1974, for example, revealed that some 30,000 workers left the Ovambo reserve for contract work beyond its borders. 9,769 of these were employed in the mining industry, 6,433 in the agricultural sector, 3,110 in government service and municipalities, 9,500 in manufacturing, trade and civil engineering, and 1,129 as servants, while 153 were unclassified.[34] Professor W. H. Thomas has estimated, however, that there were 43,500 Ovambo contract workers in the early 1970s, distributed as follows:

|  |  | % |
| --- | --- | --- |
| Mining | 12,000 | 28 |
| Modern agriculture | 10,000 | 23 |
| SWA Administration | 4,500 | 10 |
| Construction | 3,500 | 8 |
| Transport | 3,500 | 8 |
| Commerce | 3,000 | 7 |
| Fishing | 3,000 | 7 |
| Industry | 2,000 | 5 |
| Domestic Service | 2,000 | 5 |
| TOTAL | 43,500 | [35] |

While the great majority of contract workers are undoubtedly Ovambos from the north of Namibia, they are only part of the total migratory labour force.[36] Men from Kavangoland are also involved although in their case conditions in the "homeland" make the pressures to do so somewhat less extreme. For instance, according to official South African figures, which "do not include the population employed outside the homeland", the population density in Kavangoland has been estimated at 11 persons per square kilometre, compared to 52 per square kilometre in Ovamboland.[37] There were estimated to be 3,000 Kavango contract workers in 1971.[38] On the basis that they experience the same kind of restrictions on movement and discriminatory practices as contract workers from the north, the "short term" contract workers must also be included in any estimate of the total migratory labour force. A recent study undertaken for the United Nations Institute for Namibia has estimated that there were a total of 110,000 black migrant workers in 1977, of whom 75,000 came from the north of Namibia, i.e. on long-term contracts.[39] It is clear that contract labour is crucial to Namibia's booming extractive industries. Contract workers provide the main labour power for the mines; they are also central to manufacturing and the fishing industry.

Black workers as a whole undertake all the most menial and unskilled manual jobs demanded by the white economy. For 1975, the information published by the South African Department of Labour reveals that there were only 16 black people in the whole of Namibia occupying managerial, executive and administrative positions, compared with 2,164 whites. The 16 may in any case have been comprised largely if not exclusively of Coloured workers rather than Africans. Out of a total of 5,305 black workers recorded in professional, semi-professional and technical grades, virtually all were teachers (3,700) or nurses (1,600). Hardly any of the nurses had received more than a basic training, while the qualifications of black teachers in Namibia, similarly, are generally lower than those of whites within the apartheid education system. The Department's *Manpower Survey* reported a total of 1,320 black clerical workers, (compared with 6,483 whites), but it has been estimated that around 30% of these were Coloureds. Virtually all of the 2,434 black artisans and apprentices employed in the engineering, electrical, motor and building trades, were Coloureds also.[40] Until very recently there were virtually no training opportunities for black workers. (*see Table V, p. 24*).

It has been estimated that of the total African labour force in Namibia a mere 5,000 workers (about 1% of the country's adult population) have secondary education or above, while 52,500-55,000 may have complete primary education or above. Over 300,000 adult black Namibians (around two-thirds of the adult population) have no, or negligible, education. In contrast, within the white labour force, about 10,000 workers have university or other post-secondary training and a further 10,000 have secondary or equivalent education. Virtually no white workers have failed to complete primary education.[41]

While the formal "job reservation" provisions of the South African Industrial Conciliation Act have not been officially extended to Namibia, a wide variety of racially discriminatory measures, inferior educational opportunities, custom and practice on the part of white employers and obstruction by white trade unions effectively restrict black workers to unskilled, low-paid work. Black women workers suffer a double oppression in this respect. Most have little or no education and as a whole they are deliberately excluded from the majority of jobs. In general women have not been required to register as "workseekers" and are expected to remain behind in the reserves.[42] Most black women who work for wages end up as housemaids and domestic servants, laundrywomen or cleaners. Some gain jobs as shop assistants or in offices, although these are mostly

27

Coloured women. Others have been able to qualify as nurses or teachers. Black women in Windhoek and Walvis Bay emphasised:

Most of us have no education—or no formal education. We have had no school because we did not have the opportunities. We had to leave school early to go out and work to supplement the income. They are satisfied, if they can only get a job in the whites' kitchens, where they get a poor salary and have to work long hours. They are in most cases satisfied with the least . . . as a woman I have to work for another woman, a white woman. And . . . we are women with mostly big families. Because I can't do anything else, I have to clean and scrub the house of another woman who can provide me with bread, and we have many difficulties in this respect.[43]

At the bottom of the pile are those who can find no work or means of livelihood at all—and there is evidence that the number of such destitutes may be increasing. It has been estimated that between 1969 and 1977 the proportion of the black labour force (including subsistence farmers) which fell into the category "unemployed/unspecified" rose from 11.2% to 13.2%, while those "employed" in subsistence farming increased from 86,000 to 91,000.[44] United Nations sources have also concluded that the number of Africans employed in the white economy, expressed as a fraction of the total population, decreased from about 15.4% in 1960 to 12.4% in the early 1970s.[45] In an economy geared to the needs of a white minority and the demands of overseas investors, new jobs are being created at far too slow a rate to accommodate population growth. It has been deduced from data published by the South African government that less than 200 new jobs were created each year in Namibia during the 1960s, while the black labour force is currently increasing at an estimated rate of 8,000 per annum.[46] The conclusion is unavoidable—that South Africa's occupation of Namibia, and the continuing enforcement of apartheid economic policies, mean that there is no prospect of escape from poverty and neglect for the majority of the people.

## Namibia's Mineral Riches

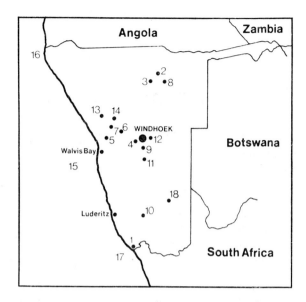

| | | |
|---|---|---|
| 1. Oranjemund | Diamonds | CDM/De Beers (*South Africa*) |
| 2. Tsumeb | Silver, copper, lead, zinc | Tsumeb Coporation (*UK, USA, South Africa*) |
| 3. Kombat/Asis West | Copper, lead, zinc | Tsumeb Corporation (*UK, USA, South Africa*) |
| 4. Matchless | Copper | Tsumeb Corporation (*UK, USA, South Africa*) |
| 5. Rössing | Uranium | RTZ/General Mining/Industrial Development Corporation/Total (*UK, South Africa, France*) |
| 6. Langer Heinrich | Uranium | General Mining (*South Africa*) |
| 7. Trekkopje | Uranium | Gold Fields (*South Africa*) |
| 8. Berg Aukas | Lead, zinc, vanadium | Gold Fields/Anglo-American (*South Africa*) |
| 9. Oamites | Copper | Falconbridge/Industrial Development Corporation (*Canada, South Africa*) |
| 10. Rosh Pinah | Lead, zinc | ISCOR (*South Africa*) |
| 11. Klein Aub | Silver, copper | General Mining (*South Africa*) |
| 12. Otjihase | Copper | Johannesburg Consolidated Investments (*South Africa*) |
| 13. Brandberg West | Tin, Wolfram | Gold Fields/Anglo American (*South Africa*) |
| 14. Uis | Tin | ISCOR (*South Africa*) |
| 15. Walvis Bay | Offshore Oil | Prospecting |
| 16. Cunene River Estuary | Offshore Oil | Prospecting |
| 17. Orange River Estuary | Natural Gas | Prospecting |
| 18. Huns Mountains | Diamonds | Prospecting |

*Source: African Business,* October 1978, p. 13.

# III

# The Experience of the Black Worker

Black workers in Namibia, like their South African counterparts, are bound by a vast and complicated net of rules and regulations. While the South African authorities have from time to time permitted some relaxation in the harshness of the system, (notably in the wake of the contract workers' strike of 1971/72 and, more recently, since the appointment by South Africa of an Administrator General to supervise Namibia's transition to independence), black workers today remain without fundamental rights.

Apartheid laws and practices, extended to Namibia since the early part of this century, have effectively stifled the emergence of a free labour market. Black workers have for years been prohibited from taking a job of their choice or from moving freely around the country in search of employment. As in South Africa, they are permitted to remain in "white" areas only on sufferance and so long as their services are required by the apartheid economy. Even then, their position is essentially temporary and insecure.

**Influx control**

Up to the end of 1977, under Namibia's version of the pass laws, any African who left his or her "homeland" to seek work in the white zone or to enter any other "homeland" required a permit, or pass, to do so. Whites, similarly, were obliged to apply for a permit to enter the "reserves" or black townships. No African workseeker was allowed to remain in any urban area for longer than 72 hours without official permission. Africans employed in Windhoek or other white areas had to carry their pass at all times showing that they were legally entitled to be there, and it had to be produced on demand on pain of arrest, prosecution, a prison term and/or a fine. As will be explained below, while these particular regulations have since been repealed by the South African authorities, a multiplicity of controls and restrictions remain to confront the black population at every stage of their lives.

Raids by the police or security guards to check up on passes, residence permits and other documentation have been a fact of life for black Namibians for decades. Homes, hostels and private property may be searched at any time without warning, resulting in mass arrests, beatings and even death. In April 1975, for example, an 18 year old Ovambo farm labourer named Johannes Sewereu was shot and killed by South African police after they opened fire on a crowd of 1,000 unarmed black contract workers at the Katutura compound, outside Windhoek. The crowd had reportedly started to throw stones at the police, who were carrying out a check on documents to find "undesirable residents". A number of other workers, policemen and municipal officials were injured. In October of that year, an inquest in the Windhoek Regional Court ruled that the police had found themselves in an "extremely dangerous position" and that the order to fire was justified.[1]

Police and employers have many means at their disposal to ensure a docile and compliant labour force. Vagrancy laws enforced in Namibia, like the pass laws, since the 1920s, allow officials to arrest Africans outside their "homelands" if they are deemed to be "idle" and "disorderly". Those who are unable to give a "good and orderly account" of themselves to a magistrate or native commissioner can be summarily removed from the area. Apart from beggars, drunkards and the unemployed, the "idle and disorderly" include anyone "found wandering over any farm or on a road crossing a farm or in or loitering near any house, shop, stable, kraal, garden etc., and those wandering about without sufficient means of support."[2] If found guilty they can be removed from the area, fined, imprisoned, or on a first conviction given the option of taking a specified job. Legislation such as this provides ample scope for the authorities to remove political "undesirables" from any area, and "repatriate" them to remote rural areas.

A survey carried out in the late 1960's in Katutura, the black township outside Windhoek where all Africans working in the city are obliged to live (Coloured people have been allocated a separate township at Khomasdal), estimated that only about 30% of the adult men could actually claim "permanent resident" status. To achieve this they had either been born in the urban area or had lived and worked there continuously for the same employer for at least 10 years (or for different employers for 15 years). The remaining 70% were merely "temporary residents"; their presence was only tolerated while they were employed and on losing their jobs they faced deportation back to the "homelands".[3] Africans who have qualified for residential status in the black townships also face dispossession from their homes if they fall behind with their rent or are involved in labour disputes. Those who have not achieved "permanent" status by the time they reach old age, even if they have been living in the urban area for many years, are "repatriated" to the homelands in a similar way. Workers employed on contracts — i.e. over half of the African labour force — can never be entitled to permanent residence in the Police Zone since on completion of their contract they are obliged to return to their "homelands".

The whole rationale of the complex legislation governing influx control and other aspects of the labour scene is to ensure that the right number of black workers are in the right place at the right time to meet the demands of the apartheid economy. Workers who are surplus to requirements can be "repatriated" to the bantustans; others can be conscripted to meet labour shortages should these arise. South African laws enforced in Namibia allow for prisoners who have not been convicted of serious offences to be hired out to public or private employers, for example. Such labour is believed to be most commonly

31

used in agriculture although little official information is available. People residing in the "homelands" whom the authorities believe to be unemployed, or "idle and disorderly", can similarly be required to undertake what amounts to forced labour on public works.

Measures such as these ensure that a continuing steady stream of migrant labour is available to employers — while wages and working conditions remain constant or even deteriorate. For the black workforce, however, the system presents an inhuman and unfeeling wall of bureaucracy and red tape. Dr. Robert Gordon, a white South African university graduate who worked as a personnel officer on a Namibian copper mine, has commented that:

The array of laws governing migration are complex, imposing, bewildering and confusing. In fact, so vague and unsatisfactory were the first set of Labour Bureau regulations in 1972 that the Government replaced them within a few months. The vagueness of these laws coupled to the fact that they have been formulated in the highest tradition of legal jargon means that few Whites and even fewer Blacks have made the effort to read and understand them. Consequently, most people accept the indubitable "expert" opinion of the Labour Officer and he is aided in maintaining his influential position by keeping both Blacks and Whites as confused as possible as to what precisely the regulations stipulate.[4]

## The contract system

Since 1972, allocation of all jobs under the contract system has officially been handled by employment or labour bureaux. These are in theory operated by the tribal authorities in the "homelands", and in the Police Zone are all headed by white employment officers.[5] A would-be migrant worker must go through these bureaux, and is obliged to accept the jobs that they offer him — refusal can mean that he is simply sent back to the bantustans. All unemployed adult men under the age of 65 in the reserves who are without severe physical or mental defects, and who cannot satisfy the tribal labour officer that they are self employed as businessmen or farmers, are obliged to register as "workseekers" at tribal labour bureaux. Each person registering must establish his identity and supply information about any distinctive qualifications that he possesses, the type of work he prefers and so on. The tribal labour officers, who thereupon classify applicants into different employment categories, possess wide powers to inquire into personal circumstances and thus wield enormous control over the lives of those under their jurisdiction — control which can potentially be used to curb political opposition to the South African occupation, and the activities of anyone attempting to organise workers in defence of their rights. In the central labour bureaux, the labour officer (in this case a white South African civil servant) keeps a secret black list of migrant workers regarded by security police or employers as "agitators". Workers on such a black list are not usually told of its existence nor offered any alternative — they are just repeatedly told that there is "no suitable employment" available. Workers can be fined up to

32

five head of cattle, or sent to prison by the tribal authorities if complaints are lodged by employers that they are "trouble makers".[6]

Once the workseeker has registered at the labour bureau, he faces the fact that, like all other migrant workers, he has been classified for life by the authorities into one of eight economic sectors — agriculture, mining, manufacturing, construction, trading, state and local authority employment, domestic service and 'other'. A worker's request to be changed to a better paying or more congenial occupation can be refused by the labour officer.[7] The worker is not able to choose his employer or to negotiate the wage for which he is prepared to work. A letter signed by a group of Ovambo contract workers in the early 70's describes the system which, in its essentials, still obtains:

> The Ovambo goes to the labour bureau and says, 'I am a driver and want work as a driver'. He is told, 'you are going to build rooms, and the pay is R5 a week'. If he says, 'I don't want building work, and I am not satisfied with R5 per week', he is chased back to Ovambo and there are no means of self-protection.[8]

More recently, contract workers interviewed in Windhoek in 1977 stressed the lack of control that the migrant possesses over his job and working conditions, his helplessness in the face of bureaucracy and in particular, the efficiency with which the system stifles the building-up of skills and experience.

> [If you leave your job] you have to return to northern Namibia and then you have to come back, with another contract. But sometimes it's very difficult to get even this contract job because sometimes if you leave a job you are going to struggle there for a year or two in order to be employed for twelve months. It's very difficult. Most workers have now been forced into the so-called homelands. In each of these homelands there is a so-called bureau for employment which is responsible for the recruitment of workers. If the worker wants to come and work here in the industrial area he has first to get a permit to visit the industrial areas. Therefore the employers are now maltreating the workers in various ways because they know that the workers are bound in the homelands — they cannot get out of the homelands any other way except through the bureau.
>
> The employers are given the right of sending workers back to their so-called homelands. That system of divide and rule, of keeping the workers divided and keeping them in the so-called homelands, is not good, because workers of the country are just workers, they are not individuals.
>
> When workers come from the north of Namibia they have to go to visit the work bureau. After they have got the documents they need to come to southern Namibia — the so-called employment area — they have to go to a certain place where they have to undress completely.
>
> And there the so-called inspectors scrutinise now . . . the parts like private parts. This is very degrading because they say if they are allowed to come to the so-called white areas without being inspected, they are going to bring diseases to the so-called white areas. I am talking about something

which I have seen. For instance, whites — tourists and so on — who come from South Africa; they are not being inspected; and there is not an office, a check point, where they have to go so that they can be asked about their passes and what nationality they are and so on. This matter has now to be examined because it is really something which is hurting the hearts of Namibian workers.

When we have arrived here in southern Namibia, we meet our employers or the people who have brought us from the [labour] bureau. Until that time a person does not know where he is going to work. Maybe he's going to work in the kitchen or he's going to work on the farm of a certain white — up to that time he doesn't know where he is going to work . . . The white chap comes there at the station and then he picks you up. He doesn't tell you where you are going to work, he's just going to say, 'you are now my boy', and he is now the so-called 'boss' and you have to go with him.

Sometimes I am told by the official labour bureau that I am going to do a certain work, but when I come here to southern Namibia I find out that I am doing [different types of] work — like today I'm a roadworker, tomorrow I am working with wires, the other day I'm painting and one day digging holes, or picking up or loading stones in the lorries, and so on. It is very difficult because a person cannot become used to one kind of work because you are doing so many kinds of work, and in the end you will find yourself knowing nothing. Once an employer dismisses me and I go to the bureau those people at the bureau are going to ask me: 'What kind of job do you do?' and I am just a worker, a general worker. There is no particular type of work in which I have specialised. And I find myself without work because those people at the bureau are only going to give work to people who are specialised in a type of work.[9]

The contract labour system has been used by the South African authorities to bolster the emergence of bantustans and the tribal authorities in Namibia. Migrant workers are required by law to return to their "homelands" on completion of their contracts, which usually last from 12 to 30 months. When a worker quits his job in the Police Zone he is given three days in which to find another. If he fails he must return to his "homeland"; if he succeeds, the law still demands that he must first go back to the "homeland" before starting his new job. If a contract worker finds a job himself and applies for permission to take it up without first returning home, he is liable to run into trouble. According to one black Namibian:

If he goes to the bureau with the paper from his old employer, or that of the new employer, the clerk tears up both papers and the man's pass. If the man has money, he is sent back to Ovambo. If he does not have it, however, he is put in jail.[10]

By convention, employers have not generally been permitted to go to the northern "homelands" to recruit labour for themselves (except in emergencies, such as the desertion of all their black workers), because this might lead to competition for labour, and "unrealistic offers of wages and work privileges".[11] It also means that a worker, on completing one contract and returning to the north before commencing another, has little chance of returning to the same employer — and hence has little or no prospect of acquiring cumulative skills and experience, wage increments, pension rights and all other normally accepted benefits of continuous employment.

Some of the more "progressive" employers, particularly large multinational companies operating in Namibia, have publicly criticised these and other aspects of the contract labour system. Consolidated Diamond Mines (CDM) for example, a subsidiary of the Anglo-American Corporation of South Africa holding a monopoly of diamond mining in Namibia, constitutes an exception to the general pattern of labour bureau operations: CDM mounts its own recruitment campaigns in Ovamboland, during which prospective employees can find out in advance about conditions and opportunities at the company's mine at Oranjemund, in the south west of Namibia. These wages and conditions are generally agreed to be the best available in the mining industry, and there is no shortage of applicants for the jobs available. According to CDM spokesmen, the company's choice of recruits is accepted without much question by the labour bureaux which process the contracts.[12] Certain other employers, notably large companies, operate a "call-card" system under which employees who have proved satisfactory, and are not too old, are given a document which allows them to return to their former jobs within a strictly limited period.

While employers may oppose particular aspects of labour legislation, they are well aware that, by and large, the system works to their advantage.

## The quality of life

A black worker in the apartheid economy is first and foremost a unit of labour, not a personality in his or her own right, with human needs and aspirations. Employers in Namibia are little different from their counterparts in South Africa in their attitudes towards their workforce. Contract workers in Windhoek described the kind of treatment that still prevails — on the part not only of employers, but the privileged white workforce as well:

When we go to work in the morning the white workers don't greet us, say 'good morning' or something like that. They just order; 'go and work there, go and do that'. But if one of them has to go and work, he doesn't know how to do it right.

Especially we workers who are working in the kitchens, we find that the whites — or our employers — think they are better than us, that they are cleaner than us. But they forget that it is we who are washing their dishes, cooking food for them, making up their beds. But when the time for eating comes they take a tin and give us food in the tin instead of in a plate. It means that those whites regard us lower than their dogs. Because when we get our food in a tin they tell us to go and eat outside, while I have to wash the plate where the dog is going to get its food. And the dog can eat inside the room while I am ordered to go and eat outside. The employers do not regard us as human beings.

Because sometimes it happens that while workers are working and one of them becomes ill, he won't be taken to the hospital because the white man is going to say 'I can't take you because the others are working', he's more concerned about the workers who are capable of working. It means that once one of them has become ill he has become unproductive, and the employer is no longer concerned about him, he is only concerned about those who are still fit to continue with the work. For black workers, the white worker who is a supervisor knows quite well that that man is sick and that it is quite possible that he can die, and he is not concerned about him.[13]

The migrant labour system, coupled with the entrenchment of bantustans in Namibia, absolves the apartheid authorities from the need to provide the housing, water supplies, roads, medical and other welfare services which would be required by a permanent labour force. Until very recently black people in Namibia were not permitted to own land anywhere in the country, and houses only in the reserves or black townships (see also below). The sick, the injured and the old are relegated to the "homelands" when they can no longer furnish labour. A recent study of labour in Namibia has commented that health facilities for black workers and their families are "thin on the ground and badly balanced between town and country, hospitals and general practice, curative and preventative medicine. Pensions are set far below subsistence. Sickness benefits and injury compensation are rudimentary. . . . And employers rarely step in where the state fails to provide.[14]

Contract workers in Windhoek in 1977 pointed out that farm workers, in particular, may have no access to any medical help whatsoever:

Many Namibian workers have lost their lives, especially those who are working on farms, because if they are ill, there is no doctor; there is nothing which is done for them. They could really have died, nobody is going to inform their families or relatives that they have passed away.

The family of the worker wouldn't know where he is. Even if he happens to die they won't know that he has died because his employer is not going to trouble himself to find out where the family or the relatives of the worker are. He's just going to keep quiet and go and buy another worker from the bureau which is responsible for the recruitment of workers.[15]

The effect of the migrant labour system on family life is one of the most traumatic consequences of the apartheid economy, both in Namibia and in South Africa. As has been explained above, African women from the northern reserves are practically never permitted to participate in the commercial economy in the south, or to accompany their husbands on contract. The majority of the black labour force live involuntarily and unnaturally as single men for the greater part of their lives while their wives and children remain in the reserves, supporting themselves on subsistence agriculture. In 1970, the adult man: woman ratio for all Africans in Namibia outside the reserves was 2:1. In 1977 it was calculated that among Ovambo workers in the Police Zone the ratio was 6:1 in the towns, 20:1 on the farms and over 490:1 in the port of Luderitz.[16] The policy, reinforced by all the other rules and regulations governing labour, ensures that workers will return home once their contracts are complete and hence the perpetuation of the migrant system. Even men who have qualified as "temporary residents" in the urban areas and are living outside the municipal hostels must wait for two years or more before being allocated houses, enabling them to bring wives and families to join them. Most men in this category live in "single" quarters or lodge with friends or relatives.

Extensive evidence of the emotional stresses and practical hardship suffered by black workers and their families as a direct result of the contract labour system has been collected by a Finnish missionary of 25 years standing in Namibia, Ms. Rauha Voipio. The results of her investigations, which took the form of a questionnaire distributed to hundreds of Ovambo contract workers and their wives, and to the pastoral workers who served among them, were published at the height of the general strike in January 1972. Letters from workers told of their suffering:

. . . God did not agree that the Christian marriage should be broken. Read Genesis 2: 18-25. We do not know why a person has to be separated from his wife for 12 months. It means much, much longing. And later the man commits adultery because of the length of the months of the contract.

Because of the contract my children do not know me. When I return home the children flee from me.

I left a small child, at home and when I return he will ask his mother: 'Who is this funny man ?' I feel depressed because of this thing.[17]

The questionnaires told of the break-up of marriages, adultery on the part of both husbands and wives, drunkenness, venereal disease, financial hardship and neglect of the children's schooling. Yet time and again, beneath all the problems and unhappiness, the replies revealed a deep-rooted desire to make the marriages work.

A major demand of striking workers in 1971/72 was the worker's right of "having his family with him, and visiting or to be visited by his family" — this is a right which the massive industrial action of that time nevertheless failed to achieve, beyond a concession entitling workers, in theory, to take a certain amount of unpaid leave to be with their families.[18] (*See also Ch. VII*). The Divisional Inspector of Labour, Mr. J. J. Badenhorst, commented at the time that this new ruling was introduced in early 1972 that the fact that this leave was unpaid and that travel expenses would have to be borne by the workers would, he hoped, prevent the "abuse" of visits home. There was some debate within ruling circles at the time over whether or not contract workers were actually serious in their demands for more contact with their families. The Secretary of the Windhoek Chamber of Commerce and of the Association of Mining Companies, Mr. Matthews, for instance, said that in his view it was entirely due to "agitation" that separation from families had been mentioned as a grievance by the workers. "The Ovambo doesn't want his family here", he proclaimed.[19] In a sense he was correct; as a white personnel officer on a Namibian mine has concluded: "Migrants would like their wives and children to visit them but are not interested in having them accompany them permanently on their work contracts even if this were legal. There are sound economic, social and cultural reasons for this and the migrants do not want their wives and children to suffer the indignities which they are forced to suffer."[20]

But the kind of reservations cited by workers about bringing their families with them on contract — poor living conditions in the townships, the prospect of losing rights to cultivate land and livestock in the reserves, the threat of summary dismissal from wage labour — reflect the insecurity and temporary character of the migrant labour system itself. What the 1972 strikers were demanding — and what is undoubtedly the continuing hope of the entire black labour force — was the overthrow of the contract system as such.

### Have things really changed?

The growing resistance inside Namibia to South African occupation, combined with international pressures, have forced South Africa to relax the impact of apartheid in certain respects. The South African government has been anxious to create the impression that it is preparing the territory for eventual independence — although the kind of "independence" that it has in mind is naturally very different from that envisaged by the national liberation movement, SWAPO, in being firmly based on racialist and "tribal" assumptions. The Turnhalle constitutional talks set up in 1975, in particular, represented an attempt of this kind — and one which quickly demonstrated the impotence of the tribal delegates in the face of the apartheid administration which had selected them to "represent" their compatriots.

As far as labour issues were concerned influx control and the labour bureau system developed into comparatively controversial issues at the Turnhalle talks. Nevertheless, a committee established by the conference to examine the workings of the pass laws was advised by a white South African official seconded from the SWA Administration that if existing controls over the movement of work-seekers into and within Namibia were abolished, this would lead to "chaotic economic and social conditions", including the lowering of wages through "uncontrolled competition", overcrowding and squatting in residential areas, crime, exploitation, intimidation, undue pressure on services and the threat of epidemics. In view of this horrifying prospect the committee, having initially intended to recommend the abolition of the pass laws, merely requested that further investigation be carried out into "the gaps which would come about if the pass laws were abolished and . . . measures necessary to bridge those gaps". It also proposed that all inhabitants of Namibia should be issued with a compulsory identity document in addition to the various permits and passes already required to be carried by the African and Coloured population.[21]

At the ruling South West Africa National Party congress in August 1976 a spokesman for Mr. M. C. Botha, the South African Minister of Bantu Administration at the time, made it clear that the government did not intend to abandon the labour bureau system in Namibia. One delegate to the congress said that better control was needed to prevent influx from the black areas and desertion by workers, and it was accepted that the system of labour bureaux and indentification documents should be improved rather than removed.[22] Subsequent events have provided further confirmation of the South African government's commitment to retaining the essential features of the apartheid labour market, while permitting reforms which, while they may appear quite dramatic, are of a superficial character.

On 21 October 1977, in particular, a number of the "pass laws" enforced in Namibia were repealed by the SWA Administrator General, Justice Marthinus Steyn. Most important, through the rescinding of eight sections of the *Native Administration Proclamation No. 11* of 1922, the obligation for Africans to carry passes and to produce these on demand was abolished. Sections of the *Natives (Urban Areas) Proclamation* of 1951, which had made it illegal for a black person to remain in an urban area for more than 72 hours without a permit, were also repealed, as were the powers previously resting with the authorities to evict unemployed blacks from the towns. Whites, similarly, would be allowed in certain circumstances to enter the reserves without official permits. A prohibition on the extension of financial credit to blacks was also lifted as part of the package of reforms.

Justice Steyn, who a few days earlier had announced the repeal in Namibia of the *Mixed Marriages* and *Immorality Acts*, took up office as Administrator General on 1 September 1977. While his official function was described as being to prepare Namibia for free elections, and to "assist in the creation and development of the new order" which would come into existence after independence, he made it clear shortly after his appointment that he was not intending to make any "fundamental" changes or to disrupt the local South African administrative set-up more than was absolutely necessary.[23] While the repeal of the pass laws was greeted as a major step forward by the South African press, it was in fact hedged about with a number of significant qualifications which continue to apply today. While Africans, after more than 50 years, are no longer obliged to carry pass books and can in theory stay without limit in the urban areas while looking for work, they may still not seek, accept or remain in employment without official permission and they must still have their contracts registered. Blacks who wish to settle away from their original place of residence can do so only if they are assured of a job. The fine for employers who fail to register their black workers at the appropriate labour bureau was increased from R100 to R300 (or six months imprisonment) at the same time as the reforms, to prevent the "new freedom of movement from degenerating into widespread vagrancy".[24]

As far as the supposed free passage into and out of the reserves was concerned, moreover, the new regulations completely excluded important areas of Namibia: namely, Ovamboland (which continued to be subject to virtual martial law enforced through emergency proclamations in 1972 and 1976); the "operational area of the South African Defence Force" (already covering the three northern "homelands" of Ovambo, Kavango and Caprivi — and hence affecting about 50% of Namibia's population; and the diamond mining areas along the south-western Atlantic coast. These continued to be "no-go areas" for anyone, black or white, without an official permit.[25]

On 11 November 1977 the emergency proclamations R17 of February 1972 and R89 of May 1976, through which martial law had been enforced in northern Namibia, were repealed by Justice Steyn. At the same time, however, he announced that they were being replaced by a special *Security District Proclamation* of his own (*Proclamation AG9*). While the new measures contained in *Proclamation AG9* were somewhat less stringent in tone, they still offered wide scope to the South African army and police to suppress political meetings and other activity.

In a press statement issued in Windhoek towards the end of November 1977, SWAPO's Secretary for Legal Affairs, Ms. Lucia Hamutenya, said that despite all the talk of ending racial discrimination in Namibia Justice Steyn had still found it necessary to retain much of the *Natives (Urban Areas) Proclamation* of 1951. SWAPO had noted, she continued, that people not in possession of residence permits or other documents were still being arrested in Katutura. These arrests followed the same pattern as they did under the supposedly repealed pass laws.[26]

Ms. Hamutenya made it clear, furthermore, that the new security *Proclamation AG9* in northern Namibia, taken together with the *Terrorism Act*, still allowed arbitrary powers of arrest and indefinite detention to the police and army. She accused Justice Steyn of continuing to endorse the bantustan policy in Namibia. What Ms. Hamutenya said merely confirmed the prediction of a senior South African Foreign Ministry official, Mr. John Viall (at that time employed in the Windhoek office of the Administrator General), who had predicted a fortnight before the emergency proclamations R17 and R89 were repealed that they would be replaced by new legislation designed to assist the security forces. Mr. Viall also said that the *Terrorism Act* would remain in force in Namibia until "peace".[27]

A recent study of labour conditions in Namibia undertaken by the International Labour Office has also pointed out that by far the most extensive provisions within the pass system were not within the original pass law (*Native Administration Proclamation No. 11 of 1922*) but in the 1951 *Natives (Urban Areas) Proclamation*, which applies to both urban areas and proclaimed areas — covering the principal urban, mining and industrial areas. Only certain sections of both pieces of legislation were repealed by Justice Steyn.[28] Many other restrictions on freedom of movement remained in force after October 1977 — the pass book was, after all, only one among a number of documents without which a black Namibian is likely to find himself or herself in difficulties with the authorities, police and army. The campaign, initiated following a decision of the Turnhalle constitutional talks, to issue all Namibians with identity cards (*see above*), for example, continued to be put into effect. In a memorandum submitted to Justice Steyn at the end of October 1977, the principals of three Damara schools in Katutura stated that it had come to their attention that officials of the so-called Identity Bureau, municipalities and even white school principals were busy with "a large-scale campaign to force Identity Books on to a large number of Blacks".[29] (According to the recommendations put to the Turnhalle delegates by the committee that had considered this matter, the proposed identity documents were to indicate the holder's "population group" by means of a code and to record name, age, address, marital status and other details, with a recent photograph.[30]) The three principals alleged that officials were using dishonest methods to circulate these documents, for example claiming that people would not be able to withdraw money from a bank or obtain a driver's licence without them, or that the cards would make it easier for them to travel to the towns. They concluded by challenging Justice Steyn to state whether or not he saw the identity documents as "another form of the pass laws".[31] SWAPO's deputy National Chairman in Windhoek, Mr. Daniel Tjongarero, further reported that certain employers were forcing Namibians to take out identity documents, or risk losing employment, while in the reserves, black farmers who refused to accept them were being prevented from selling their livestock.[32] While not directly controlling the movement of labour, it is easy to see how such identification procedures could potentially be manipulated so that their operation comes to resemble the pass laws.

These recent reforms only amount to tampering with the apartheid system and cannot meet the deeply-rooted grievances of the black population. Other measures brought in by Justice Steyn have had little practical effect. At the end of November 1977 for example, through the Native (Urban Areas) Amendment Proclamation (AG 12), Africans were enabled to purchase land in black urban areas for homes or businesses, without first obtaining official permission. They were also entitled to seek loans from building societies or other financial institutions for this purpose.[33] Home ownership schemes have been started in the Windhoek townships of Khomasdal and Katutura. Black businessmen with the capital and resources are in theory entitled to compete with whites in the industrial areas of Windhoek and other towns. In practice, however, only a tiny minority of Africans in Namibia are likely to have the means to make use of these new "privileges".[34] In the tribal reserves, moreover, the old restrictions apply, and no private ownership of land is permitted at all. In brief, since the appointment of Justice Steyn, the gross discrepancies in wealth and opportunity between whites and the overwhelming majority of blacks have remained — just as the contract labour system has continued to function.

# IV

# Wages and Fringe Benefits

Companies in Namibia's mining sector, in industry and commercial farming, earn immense profits. Yet the wages paid to the black labour force remain extremely low in comparison. While the prices of food and other basic commodities are generally higher in Namibia than in the Republic of South Africa, black wage rates are lower than their South African equivalents and the available evidence points to an even wider wage gap between black and white workers.

It is in fact very difficult to obtain satisfactory wage statistics relating to Namibia, particularly for black workers. The South African authorities do not publish series of wages or cost-of-living data, and such information as exists tends to be sparse and fragmentary. Yet in the past, before the attention of the world was focussed on Namibia, the South African government admitted quite openly that wages for black workers were extremely low. The 1967 *South West Africa Survey* for example, an official publication of the South African Department of Foreign Affairs, proclaimed that "it is neither possible nor desirable to raise the wages of all employees in less developed countries to the levels prevailing in highly developed countries and communities. Attempts to do so may result in disastrous consequences — increased labour costs may preclude the establishment of otherwise promising enterprises, hamper exports, retard the economy's rate of expansion and lead to the introduction of labour-saving techniques which seriously reduce employment opportunities".

In 1974, however, the next edition of the *South West Africa Survey* remarked that the "Territory's economic progress, especially during the past decade, has been accompanied by rising income levels for all population groups". The Survey provided wage data for Africans employed in the fishing sector and by Consolidated Diamond Mines and the Tsumeb mine. It did not mention agricultural workers however, whose wages are the lowest of all.

White employers, for their part, tend to be extremely reticent on the subject of wages. One employer approached by the authors, for example, maintained that wage levels could not be disclosed even though they had risen substantially in the last few years. The inference is that black wages are still a potential source of embarassment to the multinational concerned.

A black worker employed at a Walvis Bay canning factory by a British multinational company, Metal Box, described his situation in an interview recorded in January 1977:

> I am working for Metal Box since 1972. I started with the highest [wage]— it was then highest because I had my matric. I started with R15 a week. It

was the highest at that stage. And they did this because I have had my certificate. But in 1972 the general labourers were started with R3.50 a week, the others with R6.50 — it was the highest. . . . I have met some people who have had to look after more than ten people, but their income is just R3.50 a week.

In 1973 [Metal Box] tried to investigate the whole thing, to try to solve problems. Then after the salaries were raised, the highest was started with R12.50 — it was the highest salary in the whole of Walvis Bay. And that's why most of our blacks like to go to Metal Box to look for work, because it is one of the companies that, let us say, looks after its employees. Some of the blacks there earn more than R20 a week.

Originally the company is from England, as far as I know. They try to look after their employees. From their head office, they are interested to be the ones who are interested in their employees. But they can't always do what they want. They . . . have to go with the system.[1]

White skill and expertise can command a higher wage in Namibia than in the Republic of South Africa because conditions in the former are considered by the white community to be far less desirable. The opposite is true for Namibia's black workers; as a reflection of the poverty-line wages being paid, it has been estimated that the annual *per capita* personal income enjoyed by whites in Namibia is in the region of R3,000 per head per year, while for blacks it is a mere R125 per head per year — a ratio of 24:1. Black people in Namibia in fact have lower real personal incomes than the population of, for example, Tanzania, even though Tanzania is, overall, one of the world's poorest countries.[2]

A recent report from the United Nations Council for Namibia states that: "Most black Namibians have a negligible share in the economy. Their level of income from employment in white-run businesses is adequate only for subsistence, and does not allow for the accumulation of capital. . . . Commerce in the bantustans is handled by the South African state owned Bantu Investment Corporation whose management is entirely white. Africans are obliged to trade through this monopoly, and in this way, the sum total of African spending power is channelled back into the white-owned economy".[3]

Wage levels have in many cases risen considerably since the massive strike by contract workers in 1971–72 (*see Ch. VII*). But this does not mean that they are sufficient to meet needs or that racial inequalities have been ironed out or even lessened. Between 1971 and 1975, wages for black miners at the Tsumeb mine, for example were reported to have almost doubled from an average inclusive wage of US$63.95 per month (of which US$29.79 was paid in cash) to almost US$120 (US$64 in cash). At the same time, the average cash wage for white miners had risen from US$494.11 per month to about US$750. White miners were therefore still receiving about 12 times as much in cash as their black counterparts, plus non-cash benefits (housing, free schooling, hospital and recreational facilities) of a far superior kind.[4]

43

Contract workers from the northern bantustans are paid lower wages and remain substantially worse off than local African workers from within the Police Zone; the latter are in turn paid less than Coloured and Rehoboth workers, who themselves earn less than white employees. Women workers in all categories earn less than their male counterparts, while child workers and workers recruited from among the San Bushmen receive the lowest and most derisory wages of all.[5] Some black workers in Namibia may still receive cash wages of only R4.50 per month; others, particularly skilled and semi-skilled Coloured workers, who are less restricted in their choice of occupation, upwards of R100–150 a month.[6]

A very few black workers undoubtedly receive wages comparable to those earned by the average white. Yet for the vast majority, white expectations and living standards represent a totally different world. A recent advertisement in Namibia's main English-language newspaper, the *Windhoek Advertiser*, for example, called for a "dynamic sales representative . . . If you feel you are worth R12,000–R15,000 per annum then read on . . ." On top of the salary, "attractive fringe benefits" would include a company car, commission, bonuses, medical aid and pension scheme, and life assurance.[7] The tacit understanding was that this was an opportunity for whites.

A number of more outward-looking employers in Namibia, particularly overseas companies, have in recent years publicly rejected racial discrimination. The British based multinational Rio Tinto-Zinc Corporation, for example, maintains that it has implemented a completely non-racial wage policy at its Rössing uranium mine near Swakopmund in Namibia. Employees of all races and ethnic groups, according to the company, are graded exclusively by skill and responsibility and can look forward to equal opportunities for advancement.[8] Such an approach, however, tends to conceal the fact that the lowest paid unskilled work continues to be done exclusively by blacks while the technical and managerial salaried posts at the upper end of the scale are occupied — in practice — exclusively by whites, even though in theory they may be open to all races, (*see also p.57*).

## Payments in kind

The provision by employers of food, housing and other "fringe benefits" or payments in kind is often used by them to excuse low cash earnings. The system probably operates best in the case of big employers such as Consolidated Diamond Mines where the parent company, Anglo-American Corporation, tends to pride itself on its concern for its workforce. Educational, medical and recreational facilities may be laid on in addition to basic rations and shelter, and may indeed impress the visitor. But even here the system remains paternalistic and is often bitterly resented. Payments in kind by definition mean lower cash wages than workers could otherwise expect. Abolition of the "fringe benefits" system was in fact one of the demands made by contract workers during the mass strike of 1971–72. The workers made it clear that they did not merely seek amelioration or "a new name" for the system, but "a true contract in [the] meaning of the word", including a cash salary paid in full so that the employee "is able to buy his food and pay for his transport".[9]

Contract workers in particular are subject to a wide range of deductions and extra costs from their cash wages. They are obliged to live in accommodation provided by their employers or by the municipal authorities, as in the huge compounds in Windhoek and Walvis Bay, and to eat the food provided or go hungry. According to workers in these centres:

If you are a 'short-term' your wages are a little bit higher than that of a 'contract" because a 'contract' is provided with food — and all these things, it is decreasing your real wages which your are getting at the end.

These employers have to detract money for the accommodation and the food; and the accommodation is very bad and the quality of the food is also very rough. I know railway workers who, when they were there, were told that they were going to get R40 a month. When they arrive here in southern Namibia they find that R12 has to be subtracted from the R40 for food and R4 for accommodation.[10]

Workers have no choice about such deductions; what is more, the payments in kind that are received in lieu are often of poor quality. The food laid on for inmates in the Walvis Bay compounds, according to the workers themselves:

is very, very bad. [The workers] try to find out what they do with the money because they are getting this mealiemeal. And to make it easy for themselves they [the compound caterers] let them just eat fish, which is very cheap in Walvis Bay, they get it without buying it, and they just take a chance and let the people eat fish from Monday to Friday. . . . Sometimes the workers ask them if they can provide their own food and just pay for their accommodation but they refuse to do this.[11]

Workers complained that their non-cash benefits sometimes did not even reach them; soap for example was given away to the army. If they arrived late, they missed their meals altogether.[12]

While the quality of non-cash earnings probably has risen a little since — and, what is more important, because of — the 1971/72 strike, particularly in sectors such as mining, which are most conscious of outside observation and international pressure, it is questionable whether the improvement has been nearly big enough to contribute substantially to any rise in total earnings. To really make an impact on the quality of life not only of the individual worker but his family as well, improvements in earnings have to take the form of increases in cash wages.

**The cost of living**

The significance of any recent wage increases for the standard of living of black workers and their families must also be assessed against increases in the cost of living and inflation levels. No separate inflation figures are available for Namibia, but it is safe to assume that they would be as high, if not higher, as in South Africa itself. The bulk of Namibia's manufactured goods and a large amount of its food are imported from the Republic of South Africa, where the inflation rate has been running at more than 10% in the 1970s.

The cost of living in Namibia is higher than in South Africa, too. Peter Fraenkel, who visited Namibia in 1973, remarked that "prices of food and goods in the shops in Namibia are not very different from those in the UK, perhaps a little cheaper in general than those in European continental countries".[13] Prices vary between different parts of the country; food and other costs in the northern bantustans may be up to 50% higher than in the Windhoek shops due to the Bantu Investment Corporation monopoly.[14]

The cost of living for black workers in South Africa has often been measured by the poverty datum line (PDL) — the amount of money necessary to afford a family (usually of five) bare survival. The measure is not a satisfactory one, as its level depends on the items considered by those calculating it to be absolutely necessary, and excludes expenses such as education and medical care. PDL estimates for Namibia, moreover, are simply extrapolated from South African urban centres and no satisfactory attempt has been made to calculate them for the territory as a whole. Nevertheless, with all its shortcomings, the PDL is at least a yardstick against which to assess wage levels for black workers in Namibia.

Various estimates of the PDL have been made over the last few years. In 1973 the Windhoek Non-European Affairs Department of the South West Africa Administration recommended a minimum subsistence wage of R60 per month to support a family of undisclosed size in Windhoek.[15] Other sources put it considerably higher, at R81.25.[16] Yet in 1974 the South African authorities themselves revealed that black workers employed on the railways and in the harbours — relatively well-paid and secure jobs — received a minimum of only R48 a month.[17]

At the end of 1974 the Johannesburg *Financial Mail* gave the PDL for a family of six in Windhoek as R109 a month, a 38.8% increase over the previous year. Of the towns surveyed (the others being in South Africa itself) the journal found that Windhoek was the most expensive and its increase the steepest.[18] The University of Port Elizabeth Planning Institute estimated that the "Household Subsistence Level" (a comparable measure to the PDL) for a black family in Windhoek increased from R81.25 a month in October 1973 to R112.4 in October 1974. The HSL included only minimum rent, transport, food, clothing, heating and lighting requirements; 'decent' living requirements could be met only by a sum 50% higher.[19] A survey conducted by Adam Raphael of the London *Guardian* in 1973 showed that British companies in Namibia were paying wages well below the PDL for this period, and that wage rates were even worse than in South Africa. The report indicated that average general wages were probably around R36 a month at this time.[20]

It can be argued that families living outside the urban centres, particularly the dependents of contract workers in the northern bantustans, can supplement cash incomes with subsistence agriculture, so that these PDL calculations do not give a fair picture of black poverty. But the harsh conditions and poor soils prevailing in the reserves mean that this argument is less valid than it may at first appear; even the official *South West Africa Survey* of 1974 admitted that in bad years not even the northern areas are self-sufficient in basic food items such as cereals, and that these have to be imported — and therefore bought with cash. More recently, in March 1976, South African-sponsored delegates to the Turnhalle constitutional talks in Windhoek recommended that within one year employers should voluntarily begin to pay unskilled workers a monthly minimum cash wage of R54 and that a uniform salary scale for skilled workers should be instituted within three years. It was reported that the sub-committee which had first proposed the figure of R54 a month had arrived at it after "thorough investigation" based on the premise that wages should not be below the poverty datum line. The sub-committee also recommended that if benefits in kind were not included, the monthly cash payment should be increased to R106. Despite the Turnhalle delegates' "thorough investigation", however, the United Nations commented that the poverty datum line in Windhoek had, at the end of the previous year, been computed considerably higher, at R135.34 per month.[21]

The Turnhalle's modest proposals were almost immediately knocked to the ground by white employers, when on 24 March 1976 the powerful South West Africa Agricultural Union announced that it dissociated itself from the conference recommendations and that its members would not comply with these minimum wages.[22] Even if the recommendations had been put fully into effect they would still have lagged far behind rising costs. In October 1976 the household subsistence level for Coloured families in Windhoek was computed at R176.81 per month, while for Africans it was set at R151.14.[23] Wages in practice remained much lower. In July 1976, for example, a preliminary survey into wages received by black workers was conducted in Windhoek by Pastor Gerson Max, the Minister responsible for the United Evangelical Lutheran Church's mission to contract workers. He reported wages of R6 to R25 per month in the farming sector; R11 per month for domestic workers; R40 to R100 in the state electrical industry SWAWEK; R30 to R100 on South African Railways; and R40 to R80 per month in the hotel industry. These figures originated from employers and were not always directly comparable with those quoted by the workers themselves. In hospitals, for example, the official figure was R32 per month upwards; workers themselves said that they received 12 cents an hour, suggesting that they worked at least 60 hours a week if the R32 figure was correct.[24]

Most recently, for the period April 1977 to April 1978, the University of Port Elizabeth has calculated that the household subsistence level for a black family of six in Windhoek stood at R161.96 per month, while for a Coloured family of five it was R189.27 per month (representing increases of 7.9% and 4.1% respectively over the previous year). The claim that an African family of six can subsist on a smaller income than a Coloured family of five rests on assumptions about differing dietary habits. The University research team again concluded that Windhoek was the most expensive out of all the towns surveyed in both

South Africa and Namibia, as far as black and Coloured families were concerned.[25]

## Insurance and Pensions

As far as compensation for industrial injuries and pension rights are concerned, black workers again fall far behind whites. In practical terms, very few black workers are even covered by such provisions as exist.

A Workmen's Compensation Act, covering workers who are killed or injured through accidents at work or who contract certain industrial diseases, has been in force in Namibia since 1956. It applies to occupations regarded as more dangerous and many black workers such as domestic servants are excluded from its terms. Those that are covered are subject to built-in inequality. Compensation for severe injury and lump sum payments to relatives in case of death are calculated on the basis of previous earnings, which means that black families automatically receive less. Robert Gordon, the personnel officer of a mining company in Namibia, has reported for example that at his mine ". . . as far as I could ascertain a Black would get R400.00 for the loss of an eye, while a White would get R6,000.00 plus other sickness and accident benefits".[26] Another researcher has commented that "many men complain about the paltry compensation miners receive when involved in accidents at work, for example: if a man has been crippled at work and has received a small sum as compensation, he is discarded by the company; he has no chance of being accepted back as an employee."[27] Sickness benefits and injury compensations are not only rudimentary, but administered in such an obstructive way that they may not be taken up even where the right exists.[28] Arrangements for pensions also reveal built-in discrimination between the races. Although there is little evidence available on the exact sums paid as pensions, it has been estimated that retired whites receive roughly four times as much as Africans.[29] According to a report published by the Turnhalle constitutional conference, "employees of the same population group who are members of the same pension scheme receive the same benefits" — it is sufficiently clear that pensions differ according to race.[30]

A survey carried out by a committee of the Turnhalle constitutional conference in 1975 in fact found that only about 11.6% of the labour force was eligible for pension schemes — and only 10.7% of agricultural workers. The survey pointed out that "the most general qualifications set for membership are that the employee must fall within a definite age range, that the employee must have been in the service of his employer for a certain continuous term, or that the employee must hold his post in a permanent capacity."[31] Furthermore, "there are for the gross majority of employees no pension opportunities whatsoever." It is clear that contract workers are almost invariably excluded from these schemes: they have no control over whether or not their employment is 'continuous' — in terms of one contract succeeding another — while qualification for a scheme if it is available frequently requires prolonged periods away from home. For example, at CDM eight years of aggregate service begins to qualify workers for a pension at the age of 60 under a scheme only started after the 1971/72 strike[32] — so, to get even a minimum pension, men must spend eight years away from home, living as single men. CDM workers are lucky; other workers in the mining sector do not even get the chance of qualifying for a pension scheme. Morover, the discrimination in the Namibian mining industry against workers over 44 years makes qualification very difficult, and the eventual size of the pension, if it is earned, extremely low.

Elderly people and workers who are no longer required by the white economy are compelled to move to the arid reserves or bantustans, often leaving behind their family and friends. A woman from Windhoek, interviewed in January 1977, described their situation:

> Because I am young and strong, I can work for myself even if it is for a very poor salary. But I am very concerned about the old people of Namibia, who have a very raw deal. There are so-called homelands, to which the old people have been forced to leave. These old people have been offered a so-called old age home, which is in reality only a little corrugated room in this terrible heat of Namibia. While they build beautiful flats and houses and with lawns, trees and shade, and every possible convenience, for the white old-age [people], our old people have to live in these iron huts where they are being burnt by the sun and where they have no facilities whatsoever. It's very difficult for us because we live in the cities, and we don't know what's happened to these old people. We need a permit to visit them in the first place, then we are worried because they don't get their food regularly, although it is only porridge in most cases — most of the time their diet consists only of porridge, and we don't even know when they do get this.[33]

## Equal Pay?

Recommendations for the adoption of the principle of equal pay for equal work were made by a committee of the Turnhalle constitutional conference in July 1976. It was expected, however, that the guidelines given would be followed only in the public sector and would not apply to agriculture and the private sector. Even in the public sector, the only specific commitment appeared to be the offer of a "reasonable starting wage" to unskilled workers. Commenting on these recommendations in the South African parliament, Mr. Vorster indicated that they provided that differences in salaries and wages existing merely on the basis of colour or race would be eliminated, and that all inhabitants would be made liable for taxation on an equal basis. He implied that any reforms would be hedged around with qualifications, by saying that the practice of fringe benefits would be maintained and that a monetary value would be placed on them for the calculation of a worker's total cash earnings; that the principle of equal pay for equal work should apply for skilled workers where qualifications and experience were equal; that the salaries of skilled workers should be adjusted in phases as circumstances permitted; and that the decisions of the Turnhalle conference should not be forcibly imposed on the private or agricultural sectors.[34]

In March 1978, Mr. M. D. J. Steenkamp, Assistant to the SWA Administrator General and Chairman of a special Labour Committee set up a few weeks previously by Justice Steyn, told a press conference that he and his colleagues were presently "investigating the possibility" of introducing "equal pay for equal responsibilities". They wished to implement this as soon as possible, he continued; however, it would ultimately depend on the costs involved and whether the new independent state of Namibia felt that it could afford it.[35]

The Labour Committee's "investigations" had clearly had little or no influence on the SWA Administration, however. Shortly before Mr. Steenkamp's remarks, the Administration had decided to give all white teachers in its employ a 20% pay rise. Black teachers (in this case Coloureds and Rehoboth Basters) got extremely small increments, however. This selective pay award naturally increased the racial wage gap even further, and caused great bitterness among the Coloured and Baster teaching community. White female teachers in Namibia, with matriculation certificates and two years teacher training, for instance, received increases of R1,536 a year (bringing their maximum annual salaries to R6,750), while their Coloured counterparts received derisory increments of a mere R7.50 a year (maximum salaries R4,320 per annum).[36] (The salaries earned by the approximately 400 Coloured and Baster teachers in Namibia are of course far higher than those of the vast majority of the black workforce). A delegation of the SWA Professional Teachers Association, the organization for Coloured and Baster teachers, reported that they were told by Mr. Steenkamp in an interview that "you have waited all these years for equal pay . . . we request you to wait longer."[37]

On 13 June, two months later, Justice Steyn announced that the principle of equal pay for equal work and qualifications was to be extended to employees of all races of the SWA Administration and Public Services, including teachers and nurses. The details were to be worked out as soon as possible and implemented retrospectively to 1 April 1978.[38] Commenting on the proposed salary increases, the Secretary for South West Africa, Mr. Hennie Gous, said that while black civil servants and other government employees would gain a financial advantage, they "would have to realise . . . that there were certain responsibilities they would have to bear as well". These included having to pay the same for their accommodation and medical services as whites, for example. As a corollary of the decision on salaries, it was also announced that African public sector employees — including doctors, nursing personnel, paramedics and hospital clerks, heavy machinery operators in the Roads Department and teachers (the largest single group) — would now be liable for income tax on the same terms as their white, Coloured, Baster and Nama colleagues. Apart from a form of tribal tax paid in Ovamboland, no African had ever been required to pay income tax up to this time.[39]

In practice, this recent move will affect only a tiny minority of Namibia's black workforce. Approximately 10% of all Ovambo contract workers, for example, are employed by the SWA Administration;[40] very few if any of these are in jobs in which whites are also employed and which could therefore be said to involve "equal work and qualifications". Even in the teaching profession, one of the few areas where blacks and whites perform the same tasks, qualifications are not — in the authority's eyes and as a direct consequence of apartheid educational policies — comparable. In response to Justice Steyn's announcement, a spokesman for the Department of Coloured, Rehoboth and Nama Affairs pointed out that many teachers employed by his Department had only a Standard Eight certificate as an educational qualification, despite having many years of teaching experience.[41]

In fact, the slow pace at which the promised equal pay awards began to be implemented caused increasing dissatisfaction in the months following Justice Steyn's announcement. A letter in the *Windhoek Observer* from a health service employee for example, remarked that "August 31 provided a bitter disappointment for the black nursing staff of the Katutura State Hospital. For years there have been tentative promises of better pay . . . August's cheque was to have reflected both back pay from April, and the new salary scale. Almost predictably, the familiar old figure faced them again".[42] The SWA Professional Teachers Association, too, were reported to be "slowly becoming mutinous about the treatment they have received at the hands of the Administrator General and his Staff". They had still not received the promised equal pay for equal work by the end of October 1978.[43] Judging from an announcement by Justice Steyn, it appeared that it had in fact only been introduced by that time in the Department of Posts and Telecommunications and the South African Railways.[44]

# V
# Particular Industries

This chapter takes a closer look at the wages and conditions of the black worker in each of Namibia's main economic sectors—mining, industrial and commercial, fishing and farming.

## Mining

Mining is Namibia's most profitable economic activity, and the black labour force it employs consists almost entirely of migrant workers from the north. According to statistics published by the South African government, nearly one third of all Ovambo migrant workers are employed in the mines.[1] By far the largest single employer is the Tsumeb Corporation Ltd., controlled by United States interests. In 1973 Tsumeb employed about 40% of all contract labourers in the mining industry.[2]

Black mineworkers in Namibia undertake some of the most arduous, dangerous and unpleasant jobs going. One observer, writing about a copper mine in Namibia, has remarked that "it is difficult to imagine, let alone describe, these working conditions without actually experiencing them. To gain a small impression, try to imagine 15 pneumatic drills going full blast in a small enclosed room with a temperature of over 99° Fahrenheit and the operators working knee-deep in water and drilling not down, but horizontally".[3] While the mining industry offers some of the highest wages available to black workers in Namibia, they still lag far behind those enjoyed by whites, who occupy the most highly skilled technical and supervisory grades. "At every section of the mine there are white and black workers. Especially in manual work the white does nothing except give orders", stated a former contract mineworker. "The black is always working hard to finish all the job, including that of the boss. When loading even a very heavy thing, who does it? The Ovambo alone, while the white is standing doing nothing".[4] Another black worker on a recently opened mine concluded: "We are just helping whites to get a lot of money. You get 20 rands and he gets hundreds of rands. . . . Many whites are just people who stand behind others and call for progress."[5]

At the time of the contract labour strike in 1971–72 (*see Ch VII*), basic wage rates specified for the mining industry by the official recruiting agency SWANLA ranged from around R7 to R10 per month, plus accommodation, food and working overalls, valued at R15.25 per month.[6] Although wages for black workers have since improved, quite substantially in some cases, white wages and salaries have gone up as least as fast. While wages and fringe benefits vary quite considerably between different mining companies and different parts of the country, living conditions for the black workforce remain far from satisfactory, as an examination of a number of major mines shows.

## Tsumeb Corporation

The Tsumeb Corporation, which dominates the northern Namibian town of the same name, produces lead, copper, zinc, cadmium and silver and operates the only copper smelter and lead refinery in Namibia. It is controlled by two US companies—American Metal Climax Inc. (AMAX) and the Newmont Mining Corporation. Traditionally, Tsumeb had a reputation as an unsatisfactory employer. A memorandum submitted to the US House of Representatives Sub-Committee on Africa at the end of 1971 stated that "no African will work at Tsumeb unless absolutely forced to", and the manager of the Corporation, Mr Ratledge, admitted that "when Ovamboland has a good rainy season Tsumeb has more difficulty recruiting employees. If it's a good year and they don't have to work, they stay at home".[7] An expert on Namibia told the US Committee that she had spoken to a lot of people who had been at Tsumeb: "It had a very bad reputation. They compared it unfavourably to the wages and conditions applying to Consolidated Diamond Mines operations. For example, they were very concerned about living conditions. They say that the barracks in which they were forced to live were indistinguishable from prison, and if they tried to leave the barracks, then they were simply removed to the prison, which happened to be next door."[8]

A former Tsumeb contract worker described conditions at the mine in 1963–64:
Work began at 7 a.m. and quit at five. There was no lunch break. We ate breakfast in the compound; sour porridge, mealie bread and black coffee— it was often so bad I couldn't eat it. We got our food at the kitchen and took it to our rooms, about 14 feet square with concrete tables and concrete bunks for 16 men. We had to keep our room clean, scrubbing it down on Sundays, our only day off.

Most of the men worked underground in the mine. Others had outside jobs like watering the parks, working as houseboys for the whites, or in the mine hotels. The entire town was—and still is—run by Tsumeb Corporation; from the mines, power plant and water supply, to the parks and hotels. More than 4,000 workers lived in one huge compound. It had a high wall and only one gate, guarded by police.[9]

Statistics published by the company itself reveal that in the early 1970s, white workers at Tsumeb received cash wages on average 12 or 13 times as great as their black colleagues.[10] Even in 1975, when the giant South African company, Anglo-American Corporation, investigated the possibility of acquiring a share in Tsumeb, officials reported that
The present wages paid to black workers at Tsumeb are out of line with those paid in similar operations in Southern Africa and in the base case it has been assumed that wages would have to be doubled to bring them into

53

line. An amount of R2.5 million per annum has therefore been included in the operating expenditures to cater for this aspect. Additionally capital has been provided for in the evaluation for improved housing, recreation and training facilities for black workers.

The report went on to comment that "the black labour, mainly Ovambos, are definitely lower paid than their counterparts in South African mines...."[11]

As far as accommodation and training of black workers were concerned, the Anglo-American investigators again remained unimpressed: at Tsumeb, "the housing standards are primitive. All the hostels (for black workers) are built to a standard design with double bunked rooms each with a floor area of 42 square metres and housing 12 men (approx. 38 sq. ft. per man). Communal ablution and messing facilities are provided while the only recreational facilities are a primitive soccer field and an open cinema at each hostel area. Kombat Mine has in addition a swimming pool." Black workers at Tsumeb had little chance of acquiring skills and training, the report indicated: "no effective use is made of black labour other than as labourers, carriers of tools and vehicle drivers. Formalised training of blacks is very limited except for drivers of vehicles. All other training is done on the job." At that time the mine employed 1,339 white workers and 5,024 blacks, the latter on six-monthly contracts.[12]

In December 1977, the British manager of the Tsumeb mine was interviewed by a visiting film team. He was asked what effect Namibia's impending independence might have on his mine:

Well, our biggest problem will be keeping people here, working here. Because we cannot operate this complex without white artisans, supervisors and staff. And although we are trying to train up the Africans this is obviously something which is going to take many years. So if there is political uncertainty and we lose most of our whites then of course we're going to suffer.

*Is there any unrest among your workers—black workers, because of the political situation?*

Oh, I imagine a lot of them belong to SWAPO because most of them come from Ovamboland. But I would say that on the whole that we don't have as much unrest as you perhaps get in South Africa. The people are usually very easy to get along with—they're certainly a little more upset right now than normal but with 4,000 workers here you can expect to have some problems.

*What are you and your wife doing in this place?*

Oh, enjoying ourselves![13]

## Consolidated Diamond Mines (CDM)

In some contrast to Tsumeb, CDM is regarded as offering the best wages and conditions in the whole mining industry. The company is a subsidiary of the largest diamond company in the world, De Beers Consolidated Mines Ltd. of South Africa (itself a subsidiary of the Anglo-American Corporation). Diamond

54

mining continues to be Namibia's single most important economic activity, and here CDM has held a monopoly since 1971.

As at other companies, wages at CDM rose substantially following the 1971/72 strike. In early 1977 African labourers were reported to be earning a minimum cash wage of around R104 a month,[14] while CDM's management in London stated that black workers in the very highest skilled grades could expect to receive up to R450 per month or even slightly more. This is almost on the level of the average white mine employee. (It should be noted, however, that the highest black wages are earned only by workers employed as development assistants and the personal assistant to the labour adviser; at the most there are probably only half a dozen black workers in this top category).

These are among the best wages in Namibia and highly sought after by men on a waiting list eager to work at the mine, despite difficult physical conditions and an inhospitable environment. The diamond workings stretch about 90 km. along the southernmost coast of Namibia, northwards from the mouth of the Orange River and in a remote, arid and isolated part of the country. While the mineworkers do not have to go below ground, there are other disadvantages. The measures considered necessary to keep the theft of diamonds down to an acceptable level involves security of the most rigorous kind; recent tightening up in security has provoked complaints even from the privileged white workforce. When black workers return home they are subjected to an X-ray procedure that they find objectionable and humiliating; they must remove all their clothes, while whites have only to remove the objects in their pockets.

There are different views about accommodation and living conditions, too. According to Adam Raphael of the London *Guardian*, who investigated companies in Namibia in 1973: "Living conditions in the Oranjemund compound (they prefer to call it a hostel) bear no resemblance to the squalor of the municipal compound at Katutura. Clean, neat, single-storey buildings surrounded by trees provided tolerable quarters. The literary and technical training provided is impressive. Many of the Ovambos are now doing highly skilled jobs in the mine—in the last 10 years more than a thousand have qualified as heavy vehicle drivers. But even at Oranjemund, the problems of migrant labour have not been solved."[15]

According to a BBC television team who visited CDM's compound in early 1977, there is a very good library and common room, while some workers attained educational qualifications. Nevertheless, while otherwise praising the company, one of the visitors described the black workers' living quarters as "like seedy barracks".[16] While the notorious concrete sleeping bunks familiar from other compounds have been replaced at CDM by sprung beds covered by inch-thick felt mattresses, many of the black workers were still in 1977 housed up to 10 men and possibly more in a room.[17] A limited amount of family accommodation was at that time being built by the company to house key black workers in comparatively senior positions. (The London office of CDM informed the authors in 1977 that the company did not provide family housing for the whole of its black labour force at Oranjemund on the grounds that this would be too expensive. It had nevertheless provided family housing for 1,000 white employees at much greater expense than would be entailed by black housing units).[18] Food is provided in the company canteen as at other mines, using meat and vegetables produced on CDM's own farm; protective clothing, blankets and overalls are provided; and medical facilities are laid on.

But good physical conditions, even if they really are some of the best in Namibia, cannot compensate for lack of decision-making power and inferior status. A black CDM employee interviewed in October 1976 summed up the situation: "The working conditions at CDM: I don't say they are good at all and I say this because of the general attitude of the whites who are dominant. The law system is a hiding place for the company. The whites say we're just here on business and have no say in the apartheid law".[19] While a liaison system has apparently been set up by the CDM management to make recommendations concerning wages and living conditions, there are no trade unions or even workers' committees. CDM policy allows only one public meeting to be held at each hostel every four months, on application to the management.[20] As another former contract worker put it, "Men in this compound are jailed. They have no right to speak their problems. Men are mourning and sorrowful. Stories outside the compound say 'the people are feeling happy and all is going well!' Never!"[21]

## Rio Tinto-Zinc Corporation Ltd. (RTZ)

The Rössing Uranium mine developed by the British-based RTZ Corporation near Swakopmund has in recent years joined CDM and Tsumeb as one of the major mining concerns in Namibia. RTZ has also been one of the more prominent multinationals operating in Namibia in condemning the contract labour system, in the sense that it has made public statements on the issue. Speaking at the company's Annual General Meeting in London in May 1972 the then Chairman, Sir Val Duncan, declared that he was "totally opposed to the contract labour system and will have nothing whatever to do with it. . . . We are going to employ our labour without the contract system".[22] His pledge to have the highest possible proportion of families present, to encourage "settled communities" was repeated at the 1975 AGM.[23]

Despite these sentiments, the majority of the black workers at Rössing continue to be migrant workers employed on one-year contracts and separated from their families in the usual way. Although the uranium mine is situated on the border of the Damara 'homeland' near Swakopmund, only 700 out of a total black workforce of 1,630 in 1976 were in fact local Damaras and living in the Arandis township constructed by the company and having facilities for families.[24] The remainder were migrant workers, living in the single men's hostel or compound type of accommodation so familiar elsewhere in Namibia. This proportion has since declined further; when a team from BBC Television visited the mine in early 1977, it employed only 550 Damaras compared to 600 contract Ovambos. (The majority of the other migrant workers at Rössing are reportedly from outside Namibia altogether, namely South Africa and Malawi.[25])

In 1977 the company reported that an initial 600 family houses had been completed for black employees at the Arandis township. Arandis, according to RTZ, "has been conceived as a self-contained community in which workers from all over Namibia can bring their families to live". "The houses are of a high standard with a solar hot water system, electricity and waterborne sewage. They have four bedrooms, bathroom, kitchen (with electric cooker) and central living room."[26] Nevertheless, many of the houses were reported earlier that year by a visiting BBC TV team to be standing empty, while others had been put at the disposal of 350 single men, all Damaras. Not a single Ovambo contract worker's family had been moved in.[27]

Married white employees of Rössing live with their families in company houses and flats at the seaside town of Swakopmund. All other accommodation provided by the Rössing management in 1977 was in the form of camps or compounds for single workers only. The compounds are segregated on an ethnic basis, (for white single workers, Coloureds, Ovambos, Hereros and Xhosas) and conditions in them (with the exception of the white quarters) have been described as some of the worst in Namibia. Whereas white workers each have their own room and Coloureds share four men to a room, African workers are housed 16 to 20 men in a room, with little furniture or bedding and no privacy. The company police, moreover, are alleged to raid the black compounds in the early morning armed with dogs and sticks, and it is claimed that they take money and possessions. Expensive and poor quality food for black workers is another grievance.[28] At the May 1977 Annual General Meeting of RTZ in London the new Chairman, Sir Mark Turner, accepted criticism of 'appalling' housing conditions at Rössing, but said they were being rectified.[29]

The wages paid at the Rössing mine are comparatively high for Namibia; nevertheless, the same discrepancies between the races apply as at other mines. According to information released by Rio Tinto-Zinc at its 1978 AGM in London, Rössing employed 2,163 'hourly paid' workers, and 835 monthly paid or salaried 'staff' at 1 January 1978. Hourly pay rates ranged from a minimum of R146 per month to R559 per month. Only 23 workers were employed at this top grade however, while the great majority (over 84%) earned between R146 and R230 per month. In the salaried grades, pay ranged from a minimum of R280 per month (16 employees) to more than R1,400 per month (43 employees). Two thirds of the salaried staff lay in the range R440–R930 per month.[30]

While RTZ claims to have introduced a non-racial wages and salaries policy, and has undertaken to give equal pay to black and white workers doing the same jobs, it is clear from Fact Sheets published by the company in 1976 and 1977 that at that time all its white employees were without exception salaried staff, while all its African workers were paid on the hourly (or day-rate) scales. In 1976 a single Coloured worker had succeeded in entering a salaried grade; in 1977 this had risen to six Coloureds—out of a total of 680 salaried staff.[31]

Salaried staff in turn have access to a variety of fringe benefits, such as pensions and medical aid schemes, which are denied to black workers by virtue of the latter's contract status. Eligibility for membership of the Rössing Pension Fund, for example, is on completion of not less than 12 months continuous service with the company—a contract worker, who returns to the northern bantustans after 12 months, automatically loses any increments in wages or other benefits that he would otherwise have built up.[32]

While the wages available to black workers at the Rössing mine appear relatively high compared to those paid by other employers of contract labour in Namibia, it should be pointed out that the situation on fringe benefits is somewhat different. Board and lodging at Rössing for hourly paid workers is provided at the rate of R20 per month, deductible from wages, rather than being laid on as a form of payment in kind, in addition to cash wages, as at other mines.[33]

Conditions at other mines in Namibia, as described by a variety of observers and the companies themselves, vary—some worse in some respects, others possibly better. But the general conclusion remains, that the huge profits enjoyed by the mining houses in the 1970s, reflecting the world boom in commodity prices, have not been reflected in comparable improvements in wages and working conditions for their black employees. The massive strike of contract workers in 1971/72 served notice on mining employers in Namibia that their black workforces were not prepared to tolerate wages which, in a good month, were barely above the level of stark necessity. Nor were they prepared to put up with living conditions of a type which could scarcely be imagined by workers elsewhere in the world. Even the Turnhalle constitutional conference recognised that for a South African-sponsored constitutional settlement to have the remotest chance of acceptance by the black majority something would have to be done about the labour situation, and therefore recommended that wages should be raised. As the question of Namibia's independence has become an international issue, the mining sector—which more than any other is dominated by foreign-based multinationals—has been obliged to take a close look at its treatment of its black workers. But despite all these pressures, the inherent inequalities of the system and the vast discrepancies between the earnings, experiences and expectations of black and white workers have remained in all essentials unchanged. In other sectors of the economy, the conditions that workers can expect are even worse.

**Industry and Commerce**

At the end of January 1972, 11 African men and a Coloured student were brought to trial in Windhoek for the part they had allegedly played in organising the contract workers' strike, (*see Ch. VII*). One of the witnesses was a white foreman called Frans Voigts, who worked for a firm which ran a sub-agency for Volvo cars and sold farming equipment and building materials. Lazerus

Shikango, a 20 year-old Ovambo, and one of the accused, worked under Voigts' supervision.

Voigts was shown a contract form, marked with Shikango's thumbprint, and was asked to identify it and also to identify the accused, which he did.

"Could you tell the court how much the accused was paid?" Voigts was asked.

"One rand, 54 cents a week," he replied. There was a cry of astonishment from the black section of the court, and Magistrate Kriel reacted angrily saying he would clear the court if people on that side interrupted or made comments on the proceedings.

O'Linn waited for the comments of the courtroom to subside and put the question again, apologizing for his bad hearing.

"How much did you say you paid him?"

To which the same reply was given, "One rand, 54 cents a week."

"Did you ask him whether he had a wife or family to support?"

"No."

"Did you ask him what he was paid in his previous job?"

"No."

"Why not?"

"I didn't think it mattered," came the bland reply.

The court was seething with anger. Blacks on the benches opposite were passing back the information to the crowded corridors outside, where people could not hear the proceedings.[34]

While Lazerus Shikango's wages were probably exceptional, the incident is symptomatic of the kind of attitudes prevalent among employers in Namibia's manufacturing, industrial and commercial sectors. In 1976, unskilled black workers in the building industry, for example, could expect to receive around R28 in cash per month, plus their food. Plans were announced in May of that year by the Divisional Inspector of Labour in Namibia to introduce new minimum wage rates of around R54 per month (in line with the recommendations of the Turnhalle constitutional conference) for building and other unskilled workers. This represented an increase of over 90%. The new rates had been agreed at a conference of representatives of organised commerce and industry in Namibia. When asked whether they were legally binding the Divisional Inspector told a press conference that "there was little chance of evasion. Legal action would not be taken against employers but new contracts would not be registered unless they conformed with minimum wage scales."[35]

Even assuming the new rates had since been fully implemented, they would in any case fall below subsistence requirements, (see above p. 47). (They also excluded domestic and agricultural workers, and workers employed in the enclave of Walvis Bay). While precise information on current rates for black workers in the building industry is hard to come by, wages are known to vary from job to job. Employers who are anxious to finish a job on time may be prepared to pay wages considerably higher than usual.

A contract worker from the north, interviewed in early 1977, stated that he received R15 a month for working in a garage in Windhoek. But other workers, he said, received R10 or R12 a month, or even less.[36]

Black workers employed in the public sector can expect better treatment. In 1973/4 workers employed by South African Railways earned an average of R57 a month according to official sources.[37] The basic wages for African and Coloured railway workers were reportedly due to be increased by 12% from July 1976 and a system of annual increments introduced which would, for the first time, benefit Ovambo and Kavango contract workers.[38] Other African and Coloured public servants were also due to receive 'substantial' wage increases at this time.[39] Workers employed by Windhoek Municipality, such as black police constables and bus drivers, have also been recorded as earning in the region of R55–60 per month.[40]

Some jobs, such as shop work or clerical grades in the public sector, are undoubtedly more remunerative. But few of the migrant workers from the northern bantustans can expect to secure such posts. They have to a large extent become the preserve of Coloured workers who, while in an inferior position vis-a-vis whites, are not subject to as many restrictions as Africans. According to the 1974 *South West Africa Survey* published by the South African government, 'non-white' male shop assistants in the commercial and distributive trades earned from R170 to R240 a month, with an average of R205 in 1973. Clerical assistants earned from R127 to R235, with an average of R189 a month. Unskilled workers in the commercial and distributive trades, who are far more likely to be migrants, however, earned R55 to R90 a month, with an average of R71.

The manufacturing sector of Namibia's economy is underdeveloped, and has to compete against South African industry. The latter in fact supplies the bulk of Namibia's manufactured goods. Apart from the export-orientated mining sector, a large part of Namibia's indigenous industry is concentrated around fishing and fish canning. The two main centres are the towns of Luderitz and Walvis Bay on Namibia's sea coast. (The latter, the country's only deep sea port, is claimed by the South African government as part of South Africa and was annexed into the Cape Province in 1977). Both employ substantial numbers of migrant workers from the north, on contracts which, because of the seasonal nature of the fishing industry, tend to be rather shorter than is general in mining and agriculture—often six months. According to the *South West Africa Survey* for 1974, a contract worker at Walvis Bay could expect an average basic wage of R27.30 a month in early 1974. With bonuses and overtime his gross cash wage might reach R63.39 plus hostel accommodation and clothing. A black worker employed at a canning factory in Walvis Bay owned by the British company Metal Box stated that in 1972 he had started work on a monthly salary of R65 (the highest grade available) while general labourers earned a starting wage of about R15 a month, rising to about R28. In 1977 some black workers employed by Metal Box earned over R86 a month doing clerical work.[41]

Coloured crewmen on the fishing boats earned R100 a month at this time, while white crewmen doing the same work received R170.[42]

Domestic servants, excluded, like agricultural workers, from the new minimum wage regulations introduced by the authorities in 1976 (see above), earn some of the lowest wages. Domestic workers in Windhoek were reported in July 1976 to be earning as little as R11 per month;[43] servants in remote areas may receive even less. Women house servants in Swakopmund said in 1977 that domestic workers earned from R15 to R20 a month.[44]

Domestic workers in Windhoek, according to a former contract worker interviewed by the authors in London in 1977, were sometimes given rooms by employers who feared that the servant would be late for work if he was made to stay in the Katutura compound (see below): "And of course they don't let them sleep in the garage because they use that garage as a store room. So they have to supply them with something like a room, and if that room has a mat in it they take it out because they say you are going to waste it, and that you are not a fit person to sleep on it." This meant that the workers had nothing but a cement floor, although "some provide them with old beds". In some cases servants were given corrugated iron sheets to build shacks for themselves in the backyard.

Domestic work is in fact one of the few occupations open to women, although even here the majority of the labour force is male. It is a sector where employers can potentially find it easy to abuse the power they are given by the contract labour system. Hours can be very long, as one domestic worker pointed out:

I do all the housework, gardening, washing, ironing and cooking. I get no free time, and nothing which makes me happy. There is a terrible lot of work, but very little pay. I also work on Saturdays and Sundays.[45]

For black women, domestic service means the double drudgery of their own and their employer's household chores, with all the attendant strain and worry of leaving their own children unattended. A Windhoek woman described their situation:

We as housewives must leave our children at home during the day because there are no centres to look after our children. We have to get out and go and look for work; and if we get work then we have to start early. We have noone to look after our children, and yet we are supposed to remain content. We work for the white housewife—we have to look after her children, while we have to leave our children at home. We are forced to do this. We come home after work; we find our houses dirty; we have to clean the children now without care—they have stayed hungry the whole day. These are the problems which oppress us when we come home from work. When we come home, we don't know whether they have been to school, because they don't have a law which forces children to go to school. And we don't know whether they have eaten. Most of the time children go to the dirt-bins to scratch for food.[46]

Workers in the allied field of hotel and catering work earn more than domestic servants but here again, hours in these occupations may be excessively long. While contracts have since 1972 supposedly specified starting and finishing hours, and made provision for overtime, many migrant workers find the data insufficient to calculate the length of the working day. Moreover,

the contract mentions nothing about work on Saturdays or Sundays. A hotel servant writes, "We work from eight in the morning till 12 at night." Another says: "they tell us our wages are supplemented so that we get R27, but we weep. There is much work, and there is no Sunday and no public holiday or Saturday. We must work every day from six in the morning to seven-thirty in the evening. They say that we are working according to the contract, by means of which we came from Ovambo, but although we weep, we must work because there is nothing which can save us.[47]

In 1976, hotels in Windhoek were reported to be paying R40 to R80 per month. However, workers themselves said they were earning 14 cents an hour, a monthly salary of only about R24 assuming a 40-hour week. The discrepancy suggests an immensely long working day.[48]

As in mining, contract workers in industrial occupations are housed in large compounds or single men's hostels. In Windhoek, a new hostel scheduled to accommodate up to 5,200 contract workers and owned by the Windhoek Municipality, opened in 1978. Its predecessor, the old hostel, also housed between 4,000 and 6,000, mainly Ovambo contract workers. In the early 1970s the Windhoek Municipality charged employers R12 a month for food and accommodation for each of their workers housed there.[49] At Walvis Bay, where the municipal hostel can accommodate up to 7,400 contract workers, the charge to employers was R10.75.[50]

Conditions at the old hostel in Katutura were condemned by a wide range of commentators and visitors to Namibia. While the food and accommodation provided there were presented by the South African authorities and by white employers as a valuable supplement to cash wages, the facilities clearly fell far below acceptable standards. In 1972, for example, an American jurist, Judge William Booth, visited Namibia on behalf of the International Commission of Jurists, as an observer at the trial of alleged leaders of the general strike (*see Ch. VIII*). He paid a visit to the Katutura compound, which he described as part of "the official attempt to keep all tribes dis-united".

The men are housed in barracks-type buildings with only a concrete locker-type bed for each man. The kitchen is quite unsanitary with flies all over the place and cats chasing each other throughout the place. The food is served through openings in a wire fence separating the cooking area from the dining area. Porridge is slapped in a bowl with a shovel, a conglomeration of liquefied vegetables is poured over the porridge, and a piece of bread is also given to each man. For meat, a hunk of bone is given on which there is a slight bit of beef . . . The men also get free beer at all times. This is a specially-prepared brew which tastes not at all like our beer. It is said to be a major source of their protein. These workers come from far-off (500 miles) Ovamboland where their families must remain while the men are at work. There is no conjugal living in the compound. The area used is a fenced-off part of the black township, Katutura, six miles out of Windhoek. This township is the area designated for all black people to reside in. Inside the compound, I asked our official guide why the Ovambos were kept separated from the rest of the Katutura township and, particularly, separated from the Damara workers, who are kept in hostels on the far side of Katutura. He said that if they were permitted to live together, they would naturally fight each other to death! Later, representatives of all the black tribes heatedly denied this allegation, pointing out that Damaras, Ovambos, Hereros and all other tribes do live together in peace and harmony in the township. I couldn't help reminding myself how white America has always driven wedges in the black community by separating the "Field boys" from the "House boys", and now by separating dark from light Negroes, northern from southern Negroes and West Indian from American Negroes! I thought, too, how convenient to make a white minority superior by lumping together under the category 'white' the warring Irish, German, French, English - there, as here, creating a 'majority' which in fact does not exist.[51]

Contemporary press reports described the compound as "little less than a filthy ghetto"; "thousands of men are cooped up in a place which is totally inadequate"; "you can't expect human beings to live in that place."[52] The striking workers themselves blamed the apartheid labour system for bringing about "the erection of the compounds equalling jails with surrounding walls on top of which sharp pieces of glass are built."[53] A month before the strike started in December 1971, workers in the Katutura compound demonstrated in protest at the construction of guard towers around it. While the hostel at Walvis Bay is reputed to be better equipped, facilities at the time of the strike were similar—dormitories comprised sets of two-tiered concrete bunks, with half-inch thick felt mattresses. Striking workers at Walvis Bay complained that the beds caused lameness and death. "Why must Ovambos stay in the compound? The cross above the gate is like a sign over a graveyard. Why must we sleep on concrete beds? They freeze your blood at night and you get sick."[54]

More than five years later, conditions had not significantly changed. Workers interviewed in Walvis Bay and Windhoek in 1977 confirmed that the concrete bunks were still in use, despite frequent accidents when people fell out at night from the top bunks. Because no other space was provided workers were obliged to store all their belongings in their bunks, leaving little space for sleeping. Sixteen people were housed in a single dormitory, built in such a way that there was little chance of escape in the event of a fire, with just two small windows high up in the wall. The poor ventilation in their view caused much illness. The small windows also meant that workers had little or no chance of evading the police in the event of frequent pass raids in the small hours of the morning.

They suffered a total lack of privacy, with little or no security for their few material possessions—the police, it was claimed, frequently ransacked boxes and containers left in the dormitories, and stole the contents, on the pretext of searching for concealed knives and other weapons.[55]

Catering arrangements at the municipal compounds have also been repeatedly criticised. At the time of the 1971/72 strike, the diet at the Katutura compound consisted of sweetened porridge, bread and tea for the morning meal, with vegetables and meat for supper and half a loaf of bread with jam to take to work. The workers' own reports belie the official descriptions. A former contract worker interviewed in London in 1977, for example, stated that in the Katutura compound "they used to get offal so they got that from Damara meat packery, it's a big meat factory, and they put in bones. They throw in water and then in a big pot maize meal . . . so they've got shovels and they take the porridge with those shovels and they put it in basins." Workers formed groups of five, and each group got a basin of porridge. They had a place to eat, littered with old food. "But you see people don't eat there, they used to buy their food with the little money they got, because it's not food to eat."[56]  (*See also Ch. III.*)

Even the Divisional Inspector of Labour admitted that: "When you cook for 5,000 people you can't provide a meal appetising in appearance. You won't eat it, I won't eat it, because we are used to better. Nor do I know whether the meal is better than the Ovambo gets in his homeland. Although the meal is not appetising, it is balanced and nutritious. The same goes for bulk cooking in hospitals. If the Ovambos were allowed to cook for themselves they would not eat balanced meals."[57]

While the opening of the new hostel in Katutura has led to some improvements in living standards, all the worst features of the old system remain: housing for single men only, lack of privacy, and high walls with small windows, which led one Namibian informant to describe it as "no better than a concentration camp".[58]

### Agriculture

Although its relative importance has declined to some extent, the agricultural sector is still a major employer of labour. Official South African sources estimate that in 1970, 36.6% of economically active Africans in the South or Police Zone were employed in agriculture, (compared with 40.9% in 1960 and 54.6% in 1951).[59] In 1976 an independent researcher estimated that about 40% of the black population from within the Police Zone lived on white-owned farms, with about the same number in urban areas and about 15% in the reserves.[60] (*See also Table IV, p. 23*)

In contrast to mining, however, where the black labour force consists almost entirely of contract labour from the north, there are considerable numbers of non-contract workers in agriculture. Probably less than a quarter of all Ovambo contract workers are employed in agriculture, while it has been estimated that "about two-thirds of the regular labourers in farms in Namibia come from within the Police Zone and can live on farms with their families. According to the regional site of a farm, they are either predominantly Nama (south), Damara (central regions), Herero (central region and eastern points) or Bushmen (along the eastern border and in the far north). Some Ovambos have settled on farms as permanent labourers by getting themselves the pass of a local African, thus disguising themselves as 'Damara' or 'Herero'.[61] Bettina Gebhardt, who undertook a major survey of the social and economic conditions of farm workers during 1972 and 1973, has further commented that "definitely since the strike, farmers [have] lost interest in migrant workers, mainly because of their tendency of 'deserting' without giving notice."[62]

Farm work is in fact the last and most unpopular choice for migrant workers. The reason is not hard to find; apart from poor living conditions, the wages offered are some of the lowest in Namibia. It is only the difficulty of finding a job in the urban areas, particularly with recent rising unemployment levels, that maintains the supply of agricultural labour to white farmers. Agricultural workers tend to include a relatively high proportion of teenagers and the old; young adult men can get better-paying jobs in the mines and industry. While it is true that low wages in agriculture relative to industrial employment is not an uncommon phenomenon, in Namibia the most highly paid and skilled black agricultural workers earn wages that, at their best, are on a level with the lowest wages earned in mining.

In March 1976 the powerful white farmers' organisation, the South West Africa Agricultural Union, held a press conference to dissociate itself from proposals by the Turnhalle constitutional conference to introduce a minimum monthly cash wage of R54 (R106 without payments in kind). The farmers, clearly unnerved by the prospect of having to pay such sums to their workers, announced that they were instead preparing to appoint their own body of 'experts', to investigate and report back on the agricultural wages issue. After much prodding by reporters at the press conference, the chairman of SWAAU, Mr. A. P. Pretorius, "eventually and reluctantly" revealed the current figures. Unskilled, inexperienced black agricultural workers, he said, started with a wage of R12.50 a month, rising to R13.50 after one month. The minimum wage after 18 months service was R15.00 cash per month, plus free housing, food rations and medical services. A livestock manager (the highest grade reached by a black farm worker) earned a minimum of R27 cash per month, plus 'perks'.[63]

Another spokesman for the white farmers admitted to the press that some employers operated general dealers' or farm stores on their estates where re-sale prices were so high and wages so low that workers did not receive any cash wages at all at the end of the month—earnings had all been spent already in the form of credit at the store.[64]

It is significant that agricultural workers, with domestic servants, were specifically excluded from new minimum wage regulations introduced in July 1976 (*see above*). While South African spokesmen tend to argue that farm workers, unlike their urban counterparts, can 'live off the land' to supplement their cash earnings, some items always have to be bought—the bulk of Namibia's agricultural land is unsuitable for cereals—as do all manufactured goods. Claims made by employers about the value of 'perks' and payments in kind seem in some cases to be wildly unrealistic. In February 1977, for example, the Chairman of the Agricultural Workers Association (a division, despite its name, of the employers' organisation SWAAU), stated that the average cash wages for farm workers in beef-producing areas amounted to R24.37 per month and in sheep-producing areas to R40.37 per month (meaning, if these figures and the previous figures released by SWAAU were accurate, that quite dramatic wage rises had been awarded in the course of the preceding year). He then concluded, on the basis of his own estimates of the value of staple rations, clothing, meat and milk, housing, water and fuel, grazing rights and transport to school and the doctor, all provided by white farmers for their workers, that the wages and 'perks' of workers in the beef-producing areas amounted to a total of R83.80 per month, and to R99.80 in sheep-producing areas.[65]

In practice, the majority of black farm workers live in great poverty and under harsh conditions. Compared to their counterparts in industry and the mines, contract workers in particular find themselves in a weak and isolated position on the farms, often subject to the whims of harsh and authoritarian employers. Wages in reality may fall far below the official claims. A worker said:

Sometimes workers are told—before they leave northern Namibia—that they are going to get, for instance, R15 a month. Now if you go down to the farm where you are going to work, that farmer is only going to give you R6 a month. And if you happen to complain about it he is going to tell, Hey, Jonas, when I brought you here I brought you from the bureau, therefore I can do what I want.

*You get paid R5 a month for the work that you do?*

Yes, that's right.[66]

Contract workers in Windhoek, interviewed in 1977, described the inherent violence in the farm workers' situation:

The person has now been taken to the place where he is going to work. Sometimes it happens that he is in solitude, he's in loneliness because he's completely alone, especially when it is on a farm. Sometimes he doesn't know the way back because when he was transported he wasn't even told where he was going—he just comes to find himself alone on a farm.

If a person is on a farm, he's totally in isolation, he's isolated from other people as well as from his family or relatives. His employer won't give him the chance of writing to his family or his relatives, because that employer does not regard him as a human being. He regards that worker as just somebody to work for him.

*So you could be down here a full year and your family wouldn't know where you are until you went home again?*

Yes. Now there on the farm that farmer will force that worker to do any kind of work, any dirty work, which cannot be done by a human being. The worker has to go and look after the cattle, the sheep and goats. If one of, for instance, the sheep get lost then that worker is going to be maltreated by that farmer. He's going to beat him up or even shoot him, or he's going to let him work without getting any wages. Because the worker is alone there, he is completely powerless. On the farm he has sometimes to work for months and he is not paid.

You are being told that every morning early at five o'clock, you must come on the farm and say, 'Goeie more, baas' and then you go back. If you don't do it, you are going to get it, you are going to be thrashed.
*So every morning at five o'clock you have to go and report, just to say 'good morning'?*
You have just to say 'good morning, baas'. So no matter whether you are sick or not, you have to go in there. And you can't complain. Sometimes if you happen to be three at the farm, you don't even have contact with one another.[67]

Thomas, a Namibian who had worked on a farm in the mid-sixties, told the authors that when he went looking for his first contract job SWANLA was "very fond of taking small boys to be employed in kitchens and home jobs because these young guys were easily ordered about by women and so on." He could speak a little Afrikaans, and therefore he was very suitable "for the kitchens", and was quickly recruited. But his contract—"that piece of paper"— said nothing about wages. His job was "to do all the home jobs, everything in the house", as well as cleaning the yard. "Luckily enough in the house where I went they had a Coloured girl who did the cooking." His sleeping quarters were in the garage, "but I divided it with a piece of material, and on the other side was the car. I was lucky. Some people used to sleep just under the tree. When it was raining they were given a piece of canvas and sticks" to erect a shelter, and they had to do their own cooking outside. This testimony was borne out by Hans, Anne and other Namibians interviewed by the authors. Anne said that in most cases the only accommodation was "what we can build ourselves from sticks and bits of material", while Hans said that "workers on farms have no sleeping room, they sleep outside the owner's house." Hans was a Lutheran pastor, who travelled widely in the Police Zone to visit his 6,000 parishioners, many of them farm labourers.[68]

Bettina Gebhardt also noted that farm workers throughout the country were housed in "corrugated iron huts". In the northern part of the Police Zone where there are more trees to provide timber for frameworks, 'pondokkies', or huts made of a mixture of mud and dung, predominated. In the south, farmers had constructed cement houses. Most farmers accommodated a whole family (in the case of non-contract workers) in a single room: "In 1973 houses with more than one room for one family were found on mission farms, on Government farms and on a few privately-owned farms which had to be regarded as exceptions."[69]

In the case of food rations too, the reality is often far less favourable than the optimistic statements of the white employers might suggest. On the question of meat rations for instance, Thomas, who spoke from personal experience of contract work, stated that meat was never issued on the farms he knew, although the shepherd boys from the farmhouse sometimes stole and slaughtered one of their flock—at great cost to themselves if they were found out. Milk rations too, even of separated milk, did not necessarily reach the workers, but might be fed to the pigs instead.

The farm stores mentioned above are one example of the way in which workers can become bound to their employers by ties of indebtedness. Since 1972, under the revised contract system, train and bus fares for migrant workers have become recoverable advances, meaning that "most farm labourers and some domestic servants receive not a cent of their first month's wages".[70] Farmers may give their workers unsolicited presents, such as old clothes —and later claim them back as deductions from wages. According to Hans, now a student living in Britain who, like Thomas, had started his working career with a white farmer, his employer sometimes gave him a jacket, a shirt or a pair of shoes, and at the end of the month when pay day came but no money was forthcoming, the farmer would argue that he had "already given you so much". All the informants interviewed drew attention to the uncertainty about the size of their wages, and the fact that they never knew from month to month how much they would be paid. Bettina Gebhardt noted in her survey that "in just over half of the farms investigated [240 farms all over the country] farm labourers are allowed to buy on credit. On these farms they hardly ever get paid out their whole wage, and sometimes nothing at all. Thus some of the labourers are under financial pressure and for that reason not likely to give notice i.e. obtain a workseeker's pass."[71]

Even a committee of the Turnhalle constitutional conference which examined payments in cash and kind to agricultural employees criticised the farm store system as "it can lead to abuses. The employer can in this way exploit the employee and it may happen that he is continually in debt to the employer."[72]

'Free' grazing rights for farm workers who keep their own livestock are among the 'perks' quoted by white employers. In practice such grazing rights are only available to locally recruited workers, and migratory labour is not allowed this privilege. A former contract worker interviewed by the authors said that if such a request were put to a farmer his immediate response would be: "Do you think you are a white man?" On about half the farms surveyed by Bettina Gebhardt workers were allowed to keep a limited number of goats or cattle and a few donkeys and horses. In practice, only a few individual workers actually owned stock, presumably those in the higher, supervisory grades. "Farmers either subtract some money for the grazing when buying cattle from their labourers or they simply pay lower wages to them." During periods of drought, workers' stock might be banished from the farms.[73]

Because of the remoteness and great size of many farms in Namibia, violent breaches of human rights by white farmers may well go unpunished. Vinnia Ndadi, looking back to his own youth in the 1940s, comments in his book on the contract labour system:

> White farmers could get away with anything . . . treat their workers just as they pleased. Many times we heard about men being shot dead by their *baas* just for talking back. The law did nothing of course, it was made for the whites! We couldn't resist or even complain without being beaten or sent back to Ovamboland with no pay.[74]

Hans told the authors that he had attempted to refuse the first job offered him as a shepherd boy when he had tried to obtain contract work in 1953. For this he was jailed and fined R40. He explained his reluctance to become a farm boy, saying farm boys were often killed. He himself was often beaten up by his master when he eventually agreed to take the job. He told the authors of a case that had occurred: he had seen one of his friends killed by a farmer. The master had come back one day and found his servant had not done all the work set. He had then tied the worker to a water tap and beaten him mercilessly. When the worker died the farmer put his body in a sack, trying to dispose of it by burning. This did not succeed and the black man's remains were discovered. In this case—which had got a lot of publicity—the farmer was taken to court and eventually sentenced to nine months in jail.

Thomas was once employed by a farmer, Mr. X who was

> well-known in the area because he was a huge man, a giant, tall and big. He was well-known because some people who had contracted Ovambos were afraid to hit them, perhaps because the Ovambos were too big for them. So when one of these employers had such a big Ovambo he would call Mr. X to do the hitting, and he did—he liked it.

Thomas explained that farmers had to pay considerable fees to SWANLA for each worker as well as transport costs. Mr. X, for instance, Thomas said, would

> tell you, 'I've paid so much money for you, you have to work, otherwise I'll kill you.' I stayed two months. I couldn't stay longer because I saw him hit another Ovambo who died shortly afterwards in hospital. He hit him with an iron bar used for working a wind pump. That worker could not lift the iron bar up alone, so Mr. X hit him with it on the head, smashing his skull.

The authors asked Thomas whether Mr. X had been charged with murder. Thomas replied,

> No, no, no. There is no such thing. You see, in Namibia if a white man kills you he will have his excuses. For instance, he will say that the man he killed 'is a terrorist' or that 'he's a politician, he used to speak politics' or that 'he taught my labourers politics, he told them not to come to work'.

The police don't get their information from the dead man's fellow workers; no, they only ask the killer 'how did you kill him ?' and the reply will be, 'he was not very nice, he spoke rudely to me, so I got annoyed and hit him'.

These incidents are quoted, not simply because of their horrifying nature, but because information of this kind is contained in the evidence of very many black Namibian sources. Eminent whites such as Colin Winter, the exiled Bishop of Damaraland, have also testified to the violence and intimidation inherent in the Namibian labour system. Even a South African official in Namibia was quoted in 1972 as having told a British reporter: "You know the mentality of a certain sort of South African: if he cannot kick or beat his black men he thinks he has lost some of his own basic rights."[75]

# VI

# The Right to Organise

Industrial relations in Namibia have been described as "primitive in the extreme".[1] Black workers who seek to organise themselves to negotiate for improved wages and working conditions face a vast array of discriminatory laws and practices, official hostility, and employers who, in the case of the mining companies in particular, possess their own private police forces to suppress 'agitation'. Trade unions for black Namibians have been barely permitted to exist, while attempts to take industrial action have been vigorously crushed, leading to fines, prison terms and even to loss of life for those involved.

As is the case with other aspects of life in the territory, many of the apartheid laws enacted by successive South African governments to control black workers in the Republic have simply been extended to Namibia. While many white employees have access to recognised negotiating machinery and are represented by trade union bodies or associations, for Africans "usually the police are the first and final arbiters".[2] Coloured workers (who include Namas and Basters) occupy an intermediate position. The *Wage and Industrial Conciliation Ordinance No. 35* of 1952, the main item of South African labour legislation in force in Namibia, for a start excludes farm workers and domestic workers from its provisions. Yet these together constitute the largest group of black workers in the territory. Under Chapter 2 of the Ordinance, dealing with the settlement of industrial disputes, the registration of trade unions and conciliation procedures between workers and employers, Africans ("natives") have been expressly excluded from the definition of "employee". This has meant in practice that, until very recently, while it was not illegal for African workers to form and join their own trade unions, such unions have not been able to apply for registration and hence have not been recognised by the authorities for purposes of settling industrial disputes.

In practice, overt attempts to organise African workers into trade unions have been broken by the authorities. In 1949, the Food and Canning Workers Union, a South African trade union, attempted to work among fish cannery workers in Luderitz and Walvis Bay. Its secretary, Ray Alexander, was deported and the union suffered continual police harassment. By 1953, after at least three workers had been shot dead by police during strikes at the canning factories, its activities were forced to a halt. One or two trade unions for black workers have since been formed in the more skilled occupations (hence by definition tending to involve Coloured rather than African workers—for example a Coloured Fisherman's Union was established in Luderitz at the beginning of 1977 and accepted as such by the Minister of Labour).

A Teachers Association—teaching is one of the few professional occupations open to Africans—was founded in Ovamboland in 1970.[3] In the face of official hostility, black workers have been forced to organise informally, drawing as little attention to themselves as possible. For contract workers living in the over-crowded compounds, communication is easy; grievances can be discussed and ideas started. Workers living on white farms, or domestic servants, are in a more isolated and vulnerable position.

As far as the right to strike is concerned, white and Coloured workers are permitted under the terms of the *Wage and Industrial Conciliation Ordinance* to take such action provided that certain conditions are met—strikes are prohibited in "essential services" for example, and during the currency of an industrial agreement or award. Section 58(3), however, specifically excludes Africans from this part of the Ordinance, meaning that strikes by African workers are effectively illegal.[4] Not only strikes, but go-slows, non-cooperation and other types of action are in practice punishable by heavy fines or terms of imprisonment. The attitude of the authorities is well illustrated by Mr. M. D. J. Steenkamp, the Assistant to the SWA Administrator General and Chairman of the Committee on Labour set up by Justice Steyn early in 1978. In March 1978 he told journalists that in his view, South African labour legislation was far better than that of Britain with regard to the prevention of strikes. In Namibia, the Administrator General had the same authority as the South African government to deal with industrial action. "To strike is a crime," he added.[5]

In practice, black workers who attempt to organise face many other legal and extra-legal obstacles. The apartheid regime has sweeping powers at its disposal in Namibia, as it has in South Africa, to arrest and detain without charge, or to harass trade union 'agitators' until their work becomes impossible. Under South Africa's Terrorism Act, for example, which is applicable to Namibia and was in fact originally enacted in connection with the onset of SWAPO's armed liberation struggle, "terrorism" is defined in such broad terms as to include "prejudicing any industry or undertaking or production or distribution of com-modities or foods", encouraging "social or economic change by force or violence", or "causing financial loss to any person or the State". Under the *General law (Amendment) Act* of 1962, "sabotage" (which like "terrorism" carries a maxi-mum penalty of death) includes action calculated to disrupt power supplies, communications, the distribution of foodstuffs and other public services. Quite apart from these South African laws, emergency measures, amounting to a situation of virtual martial law, have been enforced in northern Namibia since 1972, creating further hazards and difficulties for contract workers in particular.

The complete absence of any machinery for collective bargaining means that workers are presented with their rates of pay and other conditions as a *fait accompli*. Theoretically, negotiations take place when the worker signs his contract, and the wages to be paid must be specified there. In practice, workers have little real choice—as they have little choice in selecting the job in the first place. Consolidated Diamond Mines, for example, which raises wages annually, does not negotiate with its workers the extent of the rise; this is determined by criteria decided by the company's head office in South Africa.[6] It has been pointed out that "the contracts in the fishing industry have the details [the wage rates, employers, and general conditions—particularly the length of service] printed in the open spaces, which shows the impossibility of negotiations".[7]

Before 1972, when the old contract system was still in force, employers sometimes argued that they could not pay higher wages because they were bound by SWANLA rates. (SWANLA, the "South West Africa Native Labour Association", coordinated the recruiting and transport of contract workers prior to 1972). This can no longer be used as an excuse, and in the mining industry in particular there have since been a number of wage rises. Yet such increases do not reflect a new spirit of cooperation with the workforce, but rather unilateral decisions on the part of management in the face of worker militancy and partly the influence of international pressure. Employers' attitudes in the 1970s are well illustrated by an Ovambo worker's comment that "if you ask the employer for more money, he says you are spoiled by politics". Another alleged that "the Ovambo's case is no longer being investigated. He is not questioned so that facts can come to light. He is just chased back to Ovambo. He is mocked and not heeded. Just chased away from work."[8]

The reaction of employers to the potential threat of a relaxation in labour regulations contained in the 'new deal' of 1972 (see Ch. VII) was swift; they formed themselves into associations to prevent competition for labour and to establish uniform wage rates. This move was approved by the SWA Administration and received valuable support from South African labour officials. Mr. J. J. Badenhorst, for example, the Divisional Inspector of Labour, played an 'active' part in encouraging employers to form associations in the wake of the general strike. "You must decide for yourself what is a reasonable wage", he told employers.[9] He even convened a meeting of the Chamber of Commerce, the Windhoek Municipality, the Afrikaanse Sakekamer (the Afrikaans Chamber of Commerce), the South African Railways, the Department of Posts and Telegraphs, the Master Builders' Association and other employers' representatives in the civil engineering and hotel industries to work out ways to eliminate wage competition in commerce and trade.[10] He expressed his opposition to paying more than the basic recruiting wage in the fishing industry "on the grounds that the Ovambos would see the extra one or two cents as a sign of weakness and agitate for more."[11]

White farmers in particular, in view of the low wages typical of the agricultural sector, have regularly expressed concern at the prospect of competing with mines and industry for labour. A "speciality association", the Agricultural Employers Association, was formed by the South West African Agricultural Union in 1972, with precisely this problem in mind. In 1976, SWAAU told a committee of the Turnhalle constitutional conference that "this association

73

handles all labour matters of the farming community and has since its inception approached and dealt with the labour problem with a great sense of responsibility."[12] The "responsible" employers of SWAAU later threw out the Turnhalle's recommendations on minimum wage rates, as we have seen (*see p. 47*).

In recent years a number of larger employers, particularly overseas companies in the mining and industrial sectors, have introduced their own forms of liaison with the black workforce, intended to answer the demands for trade union representation. Judging by the comments of workers interviewed in 1977, however, such innovations fall far short of what is really required. Some companies, such as Rössing Uranium for example, have set up 'works' or 'liaison' committees modelled on those found increasingly in South Africa. Such committees are intended to transmit workers' grievances to management. A worker in Walvis Bay commented:

> They have started in the factories to establish works committees, liaison committees and so forth. But if you really look at it, it's just to avoid trade unions being established. The works committees and liaison committees, they in fact do not have much power. They can only recommend, and then always it is that this matter will be taken up. But it's only to postpone the problem.
> *How are the works committees composed? Who forms them, or how are the members elected to the workers' committees?*
> It differs from factory to factory. At several factories they let the people elect their members; others are only maybe for long-service persons and it is just nominated to become a member. The secretary or chairman are—in most cases it's the manager or the accountant or someone of the management committee, and they have always got the veto right. If something dangerous etc. [arises] they say that 'No, we cannot discuss', or something like that.[13]

At Rössing Uranium, hourly paid employees (i.e. Africans and most Coloureds) are represented by four liaison committees. These are organised on an ethnic basis, one each for Damaras, Coloureds, Ovambos and Hereros—at the workers' own request, according to the Rio Tinto-Zinc Corporation management. The liaison committees comprise 12 elected members, two management representatives and a chairman from management, and meet once a month.[14]

Other companies have appointed black 'personnel managers', who are again supposed to play an intermediary role. One such concern is Walvis Bay Containers, a South-African owned firm, where a black worker described the situation as follows:

> . . . so that the people get the sense that they are represented in the management, they are now appointing personnel officers, personnel assistants, labour officers and so forth. But really I would say that the appointments of such people like personnel officers are not because the company is really interested in the welfare of the workers. It's to keep the people at ease, to give them a sense of security. It gives them a sense that someone

is representing them in the management, and so forth. And it's extremely difficult for that person to work in such circumstances. And then the other thing is—Metal Box is the first factory who started appointing a personnel officer. Every factory wants to create one now—a sort of being 'liberal'—if I am not wrong I will say that this is the second one in Walvis Bay who has been appointed, because Walvis Bay Containers and Metal Box they are just next door to one another. And the people started to say, 'Yes, look at Metal Box, they are paying such and such, which is for the people; they are doing such and such for their workers.' And then, just to be on the safe side, Walvis Bay Containers also appointed someone.[15]

It is clear from such statements that black workers in Namibia are not merely well aware of the causes and consequences of their situation, but of how things need to be changed.

The people know what is wrong. They *know* that they know. Most know where they can hit and where they can kick. But what is the protection when they hit. I think the people—the man in the street—is perfectly politically mature. The problem is the consequence of this . . . when he strikes, what will be the consequences? The danger is that the system has convicted us. We are already prisoners of the system, in many respects—say for instance with strikes. And it is our problem, we are studying this thing, because if *we* strike, what will be the consequences?

They will close the water [supply] and the people will be forced to recall their strike. Though we have enough food when we strike, the strike will only be of two days, then it's not effective. There must be preparations, and it is why I say: it is only the consequences. Our struggle is the consequences of our action . . . I observe that the people are very, very advanced and mostly when you are moving, especially in the compounds, groups are discussing only politics and what can be done and plans.[16]

Has the situation been made any easier for Namibia's black workers as a result of international initiatives over the territory and South Africa's claim to have agreed to its eventual independence? In July 1978 the SWA Administrator General Justice Steyn announced that in line with his policy of eliminating discriminatory measures during Namibia's run-up to independence, workers of all races would in future be allowed to join trade unions. Under a Proclamation published in an Extraordinary issue of the SWA *Government Gazette* of 5 July, the clause of the *Wage and Industrial Conciliation Ordinance* 1952, effectively barring "natives" from belonging to recognised trade unions, was abolished.[17]

African workers are now in theory free to join such white-dominated preserves as the Mineworkers Union, the South West Africa Municipal Staff Association, the Fishermen's Unions (Coloured and white) at Luderitz and one or two other public service associations. African trade unions can also presumably apply for registration. The English language *Windhoek Advertiser*, however, pointed out that in all other respects, the 1952 Ordinance had not changed—references to race and colour had simply been eliminated. Trade unions would

75

still, for example, have to comply with due registration procedures, and follow the rules and regulations laid down for wage negotiations.[18]

The Administrator General's Proclamation, furthermore, contained some additions to the *Wage and Industrial Conciliation Ordinance*. In particular the new legislation of July 1978 made it illegal for any registered trade union or employers' organisation to affiliate to any political party or to "grant financial assistance to or incur expenditure with the object of assisting" any political party. Vice versa, no trade union or employers' organisation is permitted to receive financial assistance from any political party.[19] While these particular amendments were not remarked on by the press at the time, they seem deliberately intended to seriously hinder the activities of the National Union of Namibian Workers (NUNW), a countrywide union organisation affiliated to SWAPO and in fact the trade union wing of the national liberation movement. NUNW has been effectively debarred from registration and official recognition. (The origins and growth of NUNW are described in *Ch. IX*.)

Only a few days before his announcement on trade unions, Justice Steyn warned those who had been distributing pamphlets in Grootfontein and Walvis Bay (urging workers to go on strike as a form of resistance to voters' registration being organised by the South African authorities in preparation for its own version of pre-independence elections) that this kind of thing constituted "treason" against Namibia and its people. Four SWAPO members were subsequently sentenced to fines of R100 each, or 12 months imprisonment (nine suspended) for distributing the "intimidating literature".[20] While it is yet too early to assess fully the impact of the new dispensation on trade union membership, there is as yet little indication of any significant change in the attitude of white workers, employers or the authorities.

The 1,000-member South West Africa Municipal Staff Association (SWAMSA), for example, applied to the Department of Labour shortly after the Administrative General's Proclamation, for re-registration to enable it to admit some 2,000 black workers who would now be eligible for membership. At the same time, however, the union proposed an amendment to its own constitution "to prevent white members being outvoted by their new black recruits". New voting and electoral arrangements were devised to ensure that a small white branch would have as many delegates as a black one.[21] White workers, in other words, were determined to remain on top.

# VII

# Resistance — The 1971/72 Strike

Industrial action by black workers in defence of their rights has a long history in Namibia, despite the great risks to individuals and their families inherent in a confrontation with the authorities. While being denied the right to organise themselves into trade unions, workers were united by their common oppression and, in the case of migrants from the north, their hatred of the demeaning contract. Strikes or threatened stoppages have occurred throughout the colonial period, although poorly documented or virtually ignored by the white population.

As early as December 1893, workers went on strike at a mine operated by the South West Africa Company at Gross Otavi. An account of the events, recorded in the diary of one Mathew Rogers, the mine manager, reveals that workers from different tribal groups joined together to make it effective. Mr. Rogers noted that he had given work to two men from the jurisdiction of Paramount Chief Samuel Maharero "paying them the usual wages with additional presents. Evidently they were dissatisfied at this rate of wages, as they refused to take it at the regular pay. During the evening, they, the Hottentot Chiefs . . . and the Ovambos conspired together to cause a general strike for increase of wages." On 5 December some workers complained to Mr. Rogers that they were being prevented from working and he promised them protection against pickets. The mine manager recorded that the blacks eventually all returned to work "when they saw my determined attitude", but on 20 December there was a further strike which resulted in a total stoppage for a few days. This strike was broken by cutting off all food rations and by sending away the "leaders of the agitators".[1]

Many strikes have taken place since World War II. According to one researcher who combed through newspaper files, the local press in Namibia reported 43 'collective actions' by Ovambo contract workers in the white-controlled industrial sector over a 20-year period from 1950 to 1971—22 on mines, five on the railways, and the remainder at Windhoek and the two ports of Luderitz and Walvis Bay.[2] Two years before this period commenced, over 2,000 contract workers at Tsumeb walked out when a 13 year-old white youth shot and killed one of their fellow workers. Heavy penalties have been imposed by the South African administration: in 1960, for example, 55 railway construction workers who went on strike at Otjiwarongo were fined the equivalent of between one and four months' wages—most of them went to gaol rather than pay the fine.[3]

Black workers have from time to time been reported to have 'deserted' their jobs—action which in other circumstances would probably have been described as a strike. In 1962 for example white farmers commented with concern that 'organised deserting' was on the increase, while SWANLA reported that there were certain districts to which contract workers refused to be sent.[4]

Employers in Namibia have had no desire to publicise poor labour relations in their factories, mines and farms, and for this reason press reports may seriously underestimate the scale of labour unrest up and down the country. The South African authorities, likewise, have been anxious to avoid international attention being focused on the disputed territory.

### Table VI Workers' Strikes in Namibia 1915-1972

| Year | Place | Other known details |
|------|-------|---------------------|
| 1916 | | Migrant workers strike for issue of working clothes. |
| 1916 | Kahn mine | Manager misleads Government in attempt to get police to intimidate workers. |
| 1918 | Farms | Workers down tools in protests . |
| 1923 | Lüderitz mines | Workers retaliate when one of them assaulted by foreman. Seventeen workers fined. |
| 1925 | Conception Bay | Strike threatened: 13 'ringleaders' arrested. |
| 1937 | Oranjemund mine | Miners strike in protest over start of X-ray examinations for pilfered diamonds of departing migrant workers. |
| 1939 | Tsumeb mine | Strike by workers who suspect not receiving pay they are entitled to. |
| 1939 | Nageib mine | |
| Sep. 1948 | Tsumeb mine | 2,000 strike in protest when 13-year-old white shoots dead one African worker. |
| 1952 | Lüderitz | Cannery workers ( ?) Large strike. |
| 1953 | Lüderitz | Fish cannery strikes; three workers shot dead by police. |
| 1953 | Walvis Bay | Fish cannery strikes. |
| 1953 | Tsumeb | Copper smelter workers strike over furnace working conditions. |
| 1954 | A copper mine | |
| 1956 | Brandberg mine | |
| 1956 | Otjisondu mine | |
| c. 1956 | Windhoek | Laundry washerwomen strike. |
| 1959 | Walvis Bay | Oceana Fish Cannery. Go-slow strike over (a) foreman's assaults and attempts to force workers to clean dangerous machinery while in motion; (b) wages; (c) 12 or 18 hour working day; (d) other working conditions. |

**Table VI cont.**

| Year | Place | Other known details |
|---|---|---|
| Jun. 1962 | Walvis Bay | Large strike; 55 arrested; fined £30 or three months jail (£30 was then between 3–9 months wages). |
| 1968 | Walvis Bay | Fish cannery workers strike, over 1,000, for over three weeks. Want night shift paid at overtime rate. |
| Apr. 1971 | Walvis Bay & Lüderitz ( ?) | Cannery strikes. |
| 13 Dec 1971– Jan. 1972 | General strike | Over 13,500 mostly migrant workers strike against whole system of pass laws, migrant labour under criminal indenture. |
| Feb. 1972 | Walvis Bay | Cannery workers against 'pig food', concrete beds and migrant labour system. |
| Feb. 1972 | Otjiwarongo | Municipal workers strike for wage rise. |

*Source:* "South Africa Labour Policy in Namibia 1915–1975" by Keith Gottschalk, in *South African Labour Bulletin* Vol. 4 Nos. 1 and 2, Jan.–Feb. 1978 pp. 90–91.

Many of the strikes in the table are recorded in the Annual Reports of the SWA Administrators. The list is almost certainly incomplete. The compiler of the table concluded that there may in fact have been over 80 strikes by Namibian workers over nearly 60 years since South African rule started in 1915.

At the end of 1971, however, a strike took place which the South African regime found impossible to conceal and which finally shook the outside world into an awareness of the plight of the black Namibian worker. It was a general strike in all but name, involving over 13,000 migrant workers and attracting unprecedented support from among the African population as a whole. From 13 December 1971 to 20 January 1972, while the strike lasted, the mining industry was brought to a halt and the communications and transport systems, farms and commerce, seriously affected. Above all the strike—the largest and longest in Namibia's history—demonstrated the potential power of the workers and their capacity to take sustained and organised action in defence of their rights. From 1972 things could never be the same again, for the mass walk-outs had made their mark on the attitudes of every migrant worker.

The majority of those who went on strike were Ovambos from the north of Namibia, and so the 1971/72 events are often referred to as an 'Ovambo' strike. But other migrant workers were involved; Kavango workers supported the strike,[5] while Herero and other leaders were reported to have urged their followers not to blackleg.[6] The objects of the strike were far-reaching: the overthrow of the entire system of contract labour and of influx control. The strikers were quite clear that their present condition amounted to a form of slavery in which workers were, in effect, bought and sold. Their grievances were set out in a pamphlet circulated and approved on 10 January 1972 at a mass meeting of strikers who had left their places of work and returned to Ovamboland. In summary, the demands were as follows:—

● the abolition of the contract labour system, the freedom for workers to choose their own employment and to change that employment without police interference. More was needed than mere improvements or a change of name. (The workers' word for 'contract' is 'odalate', meaning 'wire', a reference to the indentured terms of employment, binding the worker to his boss as if with a wire).

● the freedom to have their wives and children with them, and thus to preserve family life.

● payment of salary on merit and according to the work done, regardless of a person's colour; wage rates for all jobs should be specified.

● employees to be paid sufficient to buy their own food (rather than receive it in kind) and to pay for their own transport.

● labour offices or employment bureaux throughout the 'homelands' and in every town, with free advertising of vacancies, to enable people to look for jobs of their choice.

● the abolition of the pass book system and its replacement by identification cards.

● the government to allow many types of business enterprise, other than the 'infamous' Bantu Investment Corporation, 'which is exploiting our people'.

● the government to create new jobs and to give first preference to Africans, especially in the 'so-called homelands'.[7]

These demands were seen by the South African regime, and indeed constituted, a fundamental challenge to the social and economic status quo. The strike was thus treated as a grave political threat and met with savage repression.

There were also more immediate causes of the workers' action. One was the June 1971 Advisory Opinion of the World Court that South Africa was in illegal occupation of Namibia, a ruling which "highlighted the illegitimacy of colonial rule and the sense of impending change".[8] Another may have been that resentment had built up among workers at changes in the pass laws since the end of 1970, introducing documents with photographs rather than finger prints as in the past. The photographs made the holder much more easily identifiable, thus considerably reducing the chances of successful forgery or evasion.[9]

But the final spark that set off the strike was a remark on 15 November by Mr. Jannie de Wet, the Commissioner General for the Indigenous Peoples of South West Africa, that contract labour was not a form of slavery because the workers concerned signed their contracts 'voluntarily', without anyone forcing them. (Mr. de Wet's claim was in turn a response to growing condemnation of the labour system voiced, in particular, by the Anglican church in Namibia).

When it came, the strike call issued from Walvis Bay, where 3,200 contract workers, mainly Ovambos, were employed in the fish preparation and canning factories. A mass meeting was called and a deadline was set for the start of the strike. Delegates and letters were despatched to other centres to mobilise national support. Hinananje Nehova, a contract worker and a member of SWAPO who was intimately involved in the strike, later described what happened:

> During the second week in Walvis Bay we had a meeting with students from Windhoek to discuss our plans for a strike. SWAPO members from Walvis Bay were also present. Just about every student was a SWAPO member even though you couldn't come right out and say it. We all attended regular SWAPO meetings twice a week.
>
> Soon we began to organize. We would approach one or two workers in each factory, in the railway and building companies. We only talked to those we trusted. All agreed that something had to be done about the contract labor system.
>
> Around that time the South African Commissioner-General for Indigenous People wrote a newspaper article saying the contract workers wanted to work under the system. He said the workers came to the government and asked for jobs, never complaining that the system was inhuman. We used this article to tell our fellow workers: 'See, the South Africans are saying that we are pleased with this system, so we should do something to show them that we really don't want it. If we break this system with a strike, we could have the freedom to choose our jobs and move freely around the country; to take our families with us and to visit our friends wherever they are.' Everyone supported these ideas.
>
> In the beginning of November we held a meeting on the town soccer field. About six thousand workers from every section of Walvis Bay attended. Chipala Mokaxua, Namolo, Kamati, I and many others addressed the crowd, all saying that we should lay down our tools and go back home. We said the government had no right to interfere with our wages and that we did not need the Labor Association. We also denounced the chiefs for helping the South Africans organize the system.
>
> The reaction after the speeches was overwhelming and support for the strike swelled.[10]

(Hinananje Nehova, who was born into a peasant family in southern Angola, was subsequently arrested and handed over to the Portuguese colonial authorities by the South African police. He suffered severe torture at the hands of PIDE, the Portuguese secret service, and spent two years in prison before the fall of the Portuguese regime in April 1974 made possible his release).

On 10 December the main English language newspaper in Namibia, the *Windhoek Advertiser*, broke the news of the impending strike to its readers.

"Mr. de Wet confirmed that a strike would take place on 14 December should the plans to put it into effect materialise. On that day, hundreds of contract labourers intend handing in their contracts."[11]

On 11 December, armed contingents of South African police were rushed to Walvis Bay. On the following day, a Sunday, the authorities themselves called a meeting in an attempt to defuse the workers' growing militancy and enthusiasm. The response was clear: there could be no going back, and the bantustan officials who had been sent on to the platform were shouted down. "The crowd burst into shouting and applause, breaking up the meeting with SWAPO songs. Those who had passes burnt them in further protest against the system."[12]

On Monday morning, 13 December, the strike began. Around 6,000 workers in Windhoek refused to go to work and remained within the black township of Katutura outside the city. White schoolboys were called in to maintain essential services, but the action spread, reaching Walvis Bay, Grootfontein and the copper mines at Rehoboth and Tsumeb in the course of the week.

According to the South African government, the strike at its peak involved 13,000 workers. Unofficial estimates, however, put the number at over 20,000 —close to half the Ovambo contract labour force.[13] While the majority walked out from compounds in the towns and on the mines, a substantial number of domestic and farm workers supported the strike, despite their isolated position and the risk of reprisals from their employers.[14]

Throughout the strike and indeed afterwards, the South African authorities claimed that it had been incited by 'agitators' and 'intimidators'. In fact, the workers' actions not only revealed a striking unity of purpose and determination to carry it through, but were based on clear democratic principles. An ad hoc strike committee was set up, whose members were elected on a regional basis. The committee met for the first time on 3 January, and resolved to "reject any agreement if the strikers were not consulted and did not support it".[15] It formulated the strikers' demands, for consideration and approval at the mass meeting on 10 January (see above).

Most of the striking workers demanded to be repatriated to Ovamboland, in a bid to have nothing whatsoever to do with the white-owned economy of the Police Zone. The strike committee itself had agreed that prior to any negotiations with the authorities, the men should go back to their land and endeavour to raise as big a crop as possible, to make them independent of wage labour. Ironically, this suited the authorities quite well; it was a means of dispersing the workers and removing them—and hence the threat of open confrontation—from white industrial and residential areas. Special trains were laid on by the South African government and by mid-January, 13,500 had been transported back to their homes in the north. "We have had orders from Pretoria to get the whole lot out of here", a railway official was quoted as saying.[16]

Several attempts were made to replace the striking workers. The Assistant Manager of Railways in Namibia claimed that 124 Namas had been recruited to replace 280 Ovambos who had walked out—and that this number was sufficient to fill the gaps that had been left.[17]   Nama workers were also reported to have been despatched to Luderitz to man the crayfish packing plants, while further replacement labour was being recruited in Kavango and Damaraland.[18]   The South African Broadcasting Corporation announced towards the end of December that these "drives to recruit labour from other sources are well under way".[19] The bantustan authorities of Damaraland acted out their role as spokesmen for the South African authorities by appealing to their people to help fill the vacancies left by the contract workers and contending that "if the contract labour system was abandoned, there would be disorder on the labour market." Even they, however, agreed that changes could be brought about in the system.[20]

In general, the response of the South African authorities was an extreme one. This was particularly true of Ovamboland, culminating in the declaration of a state of emergency whose rigid conditions were only partially relaxed more than five years later, in late 1977 (see p. 40).   Large police reinforcements were flown into Namibia from South Africa. The Commissioner of Police, General Joubert, warned that the police would protect those who wanted to work.[21]   By 15 December, the migrant workers' compound at Katutura was surrounded by a police cordon armed with guns, batons and riot vehicles. From time to time individual policemen burst into the workers' rooms and searched and smashed possessions.[22]

The workers were in a state of siege, and a number who attempted to go out to buy food or on other errands were arrested and forced to pay admission-of-guilt fines.  The pass laws were also brought into play, so that the strike leadership urged the workers that "no person should give up his pass, because some brothers don't have any.  If passes are demanded, we must all refuse.  Keep on passing this message to the people.  In this way you can save those of your brothers who are in this position."[23]

Despite police intimidation, discomfort, shortage of food and the threat of heavy fines and gaol sentences, the contract workers remained resolute and united inside the Windhoek compound, until the time came to board trains back to Ovamboland.

In the north, even more draconian measures ensued.  On 14 January, the Ovambo Legislative Council (the tribal authority appointed by South Africa) announced their decision to prohibit all public meetings in Ovamboland and to authorise the South African police to arrest strikers and initiate prosecutions. By this time, thousands of striking contract workers had been repatriated and mass meetings involving the existing residents of the homeland were beginning to be held.  Resistance to the contract labour system broadened into generalised opposition to South African occupation of Namibia.  Two police helicopters and several police vehicles patrolled the border between Ovamboland and Angola after over 100 km. of the border fence had been found cut and destroyed. Several clashes with police took place, and an unknown number of Ovambos were killed and injured in the border area.[24]

On 26 January 1972 the South African government announced that the South African Defence Force—the army—were being sent to Namibia; until then the law had been imposed by armed policemen. The following day a blanket news ban was imposed in the north; no unauthorised person was allowed to enter the area, and officials were not permitted to issue statements to the press. A reign of terror ensued, in which strike meetings and gatherings were attacked and fired on, and people rounded up and arrested on a mass scale. Finally, on 4 February, a state of emergency was declared in Ovamboland under Proclamation R17 (1972).

The new regulations were summarised as follows:

> The emergency measures make it virtually impossible for any outsiders other than officials to enter the territory. A general ban is placed on all meetings. Statements likely to subvert or interfere with authority at any level; organisation of or participation in boycotts of officially-convened meetings; refusal to obey lawful orders, including orders in terms of tribal law and custom; and treatment of chiefs and headmen with "disrespect, contempt or ridicule"; all become offences punishable by a fine of up to R600 or three years' imprisonment or both. A commissioned or non-commissioned police officer is empowered to arrest without warrant and detain anyone suspected of having taken part or having intended to take part in any offence under the proclamation, and to detain him at any place until he has satisfactorily and truthfully answered all questions put to him.[25]

Despite the ban on news from the north of Namibia, information and eye-witness accounts of what was happening began to seep out. One victim of police and army operations, a deeply religious mission school teacher, later stated:

> I was locked up in a steel-barred cage with 104 other men rounded up by police at the same time as me. The cage wasn't big enough for everyone to lie down at night, so we took it in turns to sleep. There was a bucket as a latrine and dirty mealie meal porridge was thrown through the bars. We were in worse conditions than animals and not even allowed out for exercise. The police thought I had helped to organise the strike and took me away twice to beat me and give me electric shocks so I should confess. I was never charged with any offence, nor were any of the others. After 107 days they suddenly let me go. I was very weak and sick and broken hearted.[26]

"Cages" or concentration camps, were erected all over Ovamboland to hold those arrested and detained under the emergency regulations. Officially, 213 people had been detained under Proclamation R17 by 11 April, and altogether 303 in the whole of 1972, but the true total is likely to have been far higher.[27]

On 30 January 1972, in what has been termed Ovamboland's "Bloody Sunday", a group of Ovambos were fired on by South African troops as they left the Anglican church at Epinga after Mass. Four Africans were shot dead and four wounded, two of whom later died. One of those who witnessed the event, Mr. Samubua-Ehua Mualihuka, told a local newspaper that he had seen "police loading three corpses and three bodies. I also heard the report of fire-arms. When I approached, a policeman called me. I was only a few yards away from him when he started firing at me. I don't know how many shots he fired but I sustained three wounds. I had no weapons on me. I do not know why I was fired at."[28]

Bishop Colin Winter, the head of the Anglican church in Namibia (now in exile), who visited Ovamboland shortly after the incident and asked for a full-scale investigation, later released a report based on the evidence of his clergy and church members. A peaceful crowd of Ovambos, many carrying prayer and hymn books, had been returning home from Sunday church service when they saw armed South African patrols. The people

> took immediate fright and ran away from them in all directions into the bush. The patrol then withdrew . . . The African people emerged from the bush and gathered near the church. The people were discussing among themselves why the armed patrols had come when the armed men emerged from hiding and surrounded them.
>
> For the second time, the people, in fear, attempted to run away. Thereupon the police called out to them to halt. The people were searched for incriminatory documents and weapons. Eye witnesses said that the police found none.
>
> One 19-year-old African youth was carrying a walking stick. A Captain approached him and asked if he had a knife. The youth denied that he had any weapon. The Captain said, "I know you men", and was alleged to have jabbed towards the youth's head with a stick. The youth took fright and attempted to ward off the blow and the Captain fired at him. The rest of the patrol opened fire and the youth's head was splintered by bullets.
>
> The people then, again, attempted to run away and the police opened fire on the crowd and three other Africans were shot dead.[29]

According to police affidavits on the Epinga shootings, a gathering of about 100 Ovambos had refused to obey an order to surrender their weapons and disperse. They had adopted a threatening attitude and the police had opened fire. The magistrate presiding over an official inquest in June 1972 found that the police had opened fire in the execution of their duty, and that there was no criminal liability.[30]

Bishop Winter's permit to enter Ovamboland was withdrawn on 31 January 1972 and he was shortly afterwards deported from Namibia.[31]

According to the South African Minister of Police, the authorities had information that a plot had been conceived in conjunction with the contract workers' strike to murder chiefs and headmen and to attack whites, burn kraals, police headquarters and other administrative offices.[32] Strikers themselves told observers that after the police had smashed their meetings by force, often opening fire in which people were hurt or killed, workers retaliated by setting fire to kraals or killing informers.[33] For a brief period, South African government vehicles were stoned off the roads north of Ondangua, and, following the destruction of parts of the border fence, a series of attacks took place on stock control posts, inspectors and headmen. The house and business premises of a member of the Ovambo Legislative Council—the bantustan authority—were burned down by arsonists. The councillor in question had recently been appointed as the Ovambo authority's representative in the Police Zone to handle contract workers' complaints.[34] Those whom the strikers turned upon were as a rule clearly identified with the repressive labour system,[35] and the official South African reprisals were out of all proportion to the offence. Rather than open meaningful negotiations with the strikers, the authorities resorted to strong-arm tactics to crush the workers' action and to cow the African people as a whole into submission. While the South African government was forced to hold discussions and to make some concessions, they were in the long term of a superficial kind.

On 29 December 1971, two weeks into the strike, the Minister of Bantu Administration and Development, Mr. M. C. Botha, held a meeting in Pretoria with leading white officials and representatives from the mining, farming and industrial sectors in Namibia, to consider what should be done. After the meeting Mr. Botha issued a statement promising a drastic change in the contract labour system, details of which would be made known at the end of January 1972. He warned Ovambo and other African workers not to allow themselves to be misled by "agitators" in the meantime.[36]

The promised initiative opened on 19 January, when talks began in Grootfontein between Mr. Botha, white employers, officials of SWANLA, and the Ovambo and Kavango bantustan authorities. The strikers themselves were not invited—despite the fact that they had elected a deputation, which was ready and waiting for the Grootfontein talks. Commenting, the state-controlled Johannesburg radio service said that "the situation is being dealt with in an orderly and responsible way by the people directly concerned and with no interference from outside quarters. A proper settlement of this and innumerable other issues required consultation and agreement with the Ovambo people themselves." The talks were expected to be successful; if this was realised, "the credit will go to the all-black Ovambo Legislative Council."[37]

A new form of collaboration was being worked out between white employers and the South African-appointed bantustan officials to administer the contract labour system. The negotiations were cited as confirmation that the bantustan policy was succeeding in Namibia, as well as evidence that "South West Africa is well able to handle her own problems without reference to any outside organisation".[38] In fact, the close identification of the Ovambo bantustan authority with the hated contract, and its willingness to toe the official South African line, exacerbated the existing tension between the general population and the chiefs. Public statements from the Ovambo Legislative Council condemning the contract system were seen merely as exercises in public relations.

"Agreement" at the Grootfontein talks was quickly announced, and the South African Broadcasting Corporation explained to its listeners that "the negotiations warded off a potentially explosive situation in which the main objection was to the lack of negotiating rights under the old contract labour system . . . In contrast to the past, employers will have to compete for the available labour, and matters such as wages, conditions of employment and benefits will have to be negotiated. The system will also fit in more happily with the South African free economy."[39]

The main points of the amended system were that the South West Africa Native Labour Association (SWANLA) would be abolished; that in future employment would be arranged directly between employer and employee; and that it would be made easier for workers to change their jobs. In place of SWANLA, labour bureaux or employment offices, run by the bantustan authorities, were to be set up in the different regions where work-seekers could be registered and allocated to jobs. There would be written agreements— "agreement" being the new word for "contract"—which would contain details of wages, fringe benefits and conditions of service, to be furnished in a "Bantu language". These conditions would in due course become applicable to other "homelands" outside Ovambo and Kavango. Mr. Botha further stated that the new arrangements would enable workers to "maintain contact" with their families.[40]

In fact, the new labour agreement reflected, first and foremost, the discussions that had been held between the South African government and white employers, in which the latter's requirements had been outlined. There is much evidence that it was deliberately misrepresented to weaken the workers' determination to remain on strike after mid-January. The state-controlled bantustan broadcasting service, Radio Ovambo, in particular, was used in this respect. Workers told one observer that "Radio Ovambo misled the people, it told the Ovambos that they would be able to move about freely looking for jobs. The broadcasting is done by Africans, but they are monitored by white officials who speak the Ovambos' languages, and who can immediately cut off the transmitters if the announcer departs from his script." Another informant stated that "it is misleading to say there has been a change in the contract. They broadcast on Radio Ovambo that the factories want boys. We go there and find ourselves rounded up. They force the people to be recruited. We don't want to say it but what is said on Radio Ovambo is not the same as happens in Odangua" (the Ovamboland recruiting centre.)[41]

Radio Ovambo also announced that Johannes Nangatuuala, the leader of the strike committee set up by the workers, had approved of the new system and said that it met most of the strikers' grievances. Whether he was actually induced to make a statement or was misquoted is uncertain. The press, too, reported that Nangatuuala had appealed to workers to "give full support to the agreement which was reached at Grootfontein".[42] The suggestion that he had done so seems implausible, in that the agreement totally ignored one of the workers' main demands—for consultation.

The reality became clear when the strikers, impelled by the harsh conditions of the state of emergency in Ovamboland, and the need to support their families, eventually returned to contract work in the south. The system of labour repression was found to be unchanged in all essentials. Conditions in the municipal compound at Katutura, in particular, were the same as ever—and if anything, worse, since the 80 cleaners in the compound had also gone on strike and nothing had been done to clear up the debris from the workers' occupation and the police raids. Many of the returning workers refused to sleep in the compound; 2,000 refused medical examinations; strong complaints were made about the standard of rations and accommodation. In their frustration and anger, the men smashed 4,000 of the 6,000 concrete "beds" in the compound and did extensive damage to the buildings.[43] Dissatisfaction was evident even before the workers reached their destinations in the Police Zone; on registration many refused the rations offered them; many refused to be photographed; others demanded buses or taxis instead of the trucks usually provided for their transport.

In Walvis Bay, several hundred contract workers walked out of their jobs when they were refused overtime pay for night work at the fish factories. They also complained about food and accommodation. According to the police, there were no incidents, and strikers waited "calmly and peacefully" for a reply to their demands.[44] White attitudes remained intransigent, however: in appealing for "firm action" to be taken in the event of a strike or damage to property, the Mayor of Walvis Bay, Dr. Laubser, complained that the Ovambos were beginning to lose respect for the white man. His plan called for the granting of more power to the police and urged the government to pay less attention to international opinion in dealing with the Ovambo labour problem.[45]

By April 1972, things were still not back to normal. A correspondent reported: "The labour situation in South West Africa three months after the strike is still unsettled, with hundreds of workers still not back at work. A State of Emergency is still in force in Ovamboland, where most of the workers come from."[46] Repression continued, concealed from the outside world by the South African government's news black-out.

In terms of actual gains, the workers won, in some cases, higher wages although some claimed to have been deceived even on this point, and that the money had not been paid. It has been calculated that actual cash wages rose by an average of between one-tenth and one-fifth for migrant workers, while the minimum wages paid rose more. This had to be offset, however, against increases in the cost of living, plus the fact that, under the new agreement, employers were no longer obliged to supply their workers with clothes or to pay for their return journey on completion of the contract.[47] While a welcome move away from paternalism, these changes implied financial hardship for the workers. "According to the agreement, train and bus fares are recoverable advances. The bus fare from Ondangwa to Grootfontein is R3.60 (for farmworkers R1.20) and the train journey to Walvis Bay costs R6.41. This means that most farm labourers and some domestic servants receive not a cent of their first month's wages." Similarly, "Before the strike each contract-Ovambo at Grootfontein was given a khaki shirt and shorts. Previously some factories (for example those in Walvis Bay) gave jam and tobacco or sweets to workers once a weeek. These privileges have been stopped because of increased wages. Where there has been no raise, or where it has been only nominal, this loss is regarded as an injustice."[48]

Other gains included paid leave at the end of the contract and entitlement to unpaid home leave during the service period. Breach of contract became a civil rather than a criminal offence. Workers could resign a job, provided they meticulously followed the detailed legal procedure, and legally take up a better-paid or less arduous job—provided they could find one. Even these concessions were hedged about with bureaucratic rules and regulations. Africans breaching their contracts might find themselves blacklisted by the labour bureaux and unable to obtain permits to look for other jobs.[49]

As one observer has concluded:

> Above all, while there was much cosmetic tinkering ("masters" and "servants" became "employers" and "employees", "compounds" were renamed "hostels", "deserters" were mitigated into merely "absconders", and the "Ovambo native tribes" and "Okovango native tribes" were constitutionally transmigrated into the "Ovambo" and "Kavango Bantu nations") migrant workers were not permitted to settle permanently at their places of employment, could still not be accompanied by their wives and families, and still had to live in "men-only" compounds.
>
> Increased police pass raids, new "control gates" on compounds, and new photo-identity documents made it possible for the authorities to enforce the pass and migrant system more efficiently than before. In short, there was no abolition of the migrant labour system, merely an updating of it and a "new name for wire".[50]

The attitudes of the contract workers' white employers remained largely unchanged. On 1 March 1972, for example, the General Manager of the Tsumeb mine was quoted as saying (despite the experience of the strike) that: "I do not subscribe to the attitude that if a company—by its initiative, skills and so on—is making big profits, it is necessary to contribute them to labour."[51]

The greatest impact of the strike of 1971/72 was on the workers themselves. It increased the militancy and self-confidence of the black population, and made it clear to the whites that constitutional change of some sort had to come. The immediate response of the South African government was to accelerate its programme of "indirect rule" for Namibia (i.e. the establishment of "self-governing" bantustans) as well as to make cosmetic changes in the contract labour system itself. The apartheid authorities were well aware that the experience of the strike could only serve to reinforce the wider struggle against South Africa's occupation and for national liberation.

# VIII

# The Apartheid Response —
# Divide and Rule

In June 1972, eight out of 12 men accused of leading the general strike of six months before were found guilty as charged in the Windhoek Regional Court. They had been accused of intimidating other workers and inciting them to strike by threats of violence, and of breaking their own labour contracts by striking. The eight, all Ovambos, were each sentenced to a fine of R25 (or 25 days in gaol), and two months imprisonment, suspended for three years. Three more contract workers from Ovamboland, and a Coloured student, were acquitted. The men had first appeared in court on 25 January 1972, and their trial like the strike itself had attracted worldwide attention. Two British MPs and a judge from the United States had sat in on the proceedings as observers for the International Commission of Jurists, and their presence had undoubtedly made an impression on the presiding magistrate, Mr. H. J. Kriel, who decided on an appropriate sentence. In his comments on the case, Mr. Kriel said that "when one takes the rising cost-of-living into consideration, it is difficult to imagine how someone could make do and remain satisfied with so little money." He added that the strike had made most employers realise that their workers were underpaid.[1]

As far as Namibia's black workers themselves were concerned, much had been learned from the strike. There was a new spirit of self-confidence among the many thousands who had been involved, which in turn affected others. Namibians were determined to continue their resistance to exploitation in the work place, if necessary by other means. While the events of 1971/72 did not lead to any fundamental change in the contract labour system, they clarified many people's perceptions of South Africa's apartheid strategy and led to a sharpening of opposition to the tribal authorities. Increasingly the black Namibians appointed to positions in the "homeland" governments were seen to be collaborating with the South African authorities in operating the contract system. Workers recorded by Ms. Ruaha Voipio in the months following the strike said, for example, that

> The contract is a very bad thing, but it has been forced upon us by our headmen.

> Our headmen in Ovambo trouble us in their collaboration with whites, because they have good jobs and are paid enough. They no longer look after their people, their children, but have turned their backs on us, and give us a snake when we ask for fish.[2]

90

Over the seven years since the general strike, South Africa has made strenuous efforts to entrench tribalism and racial difference in Namibia. While it has certainly been prepared, under pressure, to remove some of the more blatant manifestations of apartheid such as the *Mixed Marriages* and *Immorality Acts*, and to allow black Namibians to enter hotels and other public places previously reserved for whites, the South African government has consistently followed an "ethnic" strategy for Namibia's eventual independence. It has maintained that only through their respective "population groups" can the Namibian people hope to achieve full self-determination and national identity. The Turnhalle constitutional talks, convened by South Africa in 1975 in response to the growing momentum of armed guerilla struggle in northern Namibia and mounting demands at the United Nations for the territory's independence, comprised hand-picked tribal delegations from each of 12 "population groups", including whites. Here in fact was the Odendaal apartheid blueprint in miniature and, not surprisingly, the Turnhalle in due course came up with an independence constitution based on the existing system of ultimately "self-governing" bantustans or tribal reserves.[3]

While the impression has been spread that the Turnhalle's plans were suspended by South Africa in 1977 pending negotiations with the five Western members of the United Nations Security Council and the appointment by the South African government of an Administrator General to supervise Namibia's transition to independence, the apartheid principles on which they were based are still very much alive. During 1978, in particular, the Democratic Turnhalle Alliance, a political party formed out of the delegations to the Turnhalle talks, received massive backing in the form of funds, media coverage and official approval during the run-up to South African-sponsored general elections. Concerted efforts continue to be made to use tribal differences to weaken and divide organised resistance to South African occupation—a strategy with which the black workforce, whose day-to-day existence is governed by racial laws, is only too familiar.

There has been a number of examples of industrial action inside Namibia since 1972, some on quite a large scale. They have generally received little publicity and at best have been presented in a confused and distorted manner by the South African authorities. Workers who have taken strike action have continued to be met with official hostility and the threat, if not the reality, of violence. In November 1976, for example, eight truck-loads of South African riot police were reported to have been moved into the Rössing Uranium mine near Swakopmund, as a back-up force for the company's own private police in case of "trouble".[4] The strike, which was reported in the British press, constituted an obvious source of embarrassment to the British parent company concerned, the Rio Tinto-Zinc Corporation. RTZ, as has already been indicated, prides itself on the labour relations prevailing at the Rössing plant.[5]

On the previous day, 18 November 1976, Damara workers at the Rössing mine, who then numbered about 700 out of a total black workforce of 1700, had walked out following complaints about the poor quality and high cost of the food supplied in the company canteens. The general manager of the mine, Mr. Richard Hughes, said that workers had also objected to a rule forbidding them to take food out of the canteen for their families at the married quarters in the mine township of Arandis.[6] Many workers may in fact have had difficulty in keeping to the canteen's opening times due to long and irregular hours of work, despite having to pay just under a fifth of their average monthly wage on company food, whether eaten or not.[7] Compared to white and Coloured workers the Damara and other African workers seem to have had little choice or variety in a diet of maize porridge, meat, bread and lemons or apples.[8] There were other grievances besides. Medical checks for whites had increased in frequency after three white mine employees had registered high radioactive readings, and the Damaras alleged that the company cared more about the health of whites than blacks.[9]

Two days after the onset of the strike, RTZ's general manager for personnel and external relations in Southern Africa, Mr. Fred Stiglingh, said that following unsuccessful attempts to negotiate, the Damara workers would be replaced or dismissed if they did not return to work.[10] In the event the strike—which had at no time involved the Ovambo contract workers at Rössing—lasted for five days. Mine officials agreed to meet the Damara representatives to discuss the situation while Mr. Stiglingh, in some contrast to his earlier remarks, was reported as saying that "as far as he was concerned, the men were free to strike and he was quite prepared to talk to them about their grievances."[11]

The Rössing management has been accused of using divisive tactics in dealing with the workforce, and playing off one group against another, using privileges or differential pay. Black workers at Rössing, interviewed a few weeks after the strike, reported that the company's original policy of giving preference to Damara job seekers (a policy linked to the professed aim of RTZ to phase out the contract system)[12] seemed to have been abandoned in the wake of the strike. Ovambo applicants were now more likely to be taken on. The management was more nervous. According to one worker:

the employers . . . fear that these people will somehow in the near future have another strike because this awareness of knowing which is right and which is wrong, seeing that this thing is not right, that is wrong with food and the conditions where they are staying and discovering all that . . . they see it from the first experience when they had the first strike.[13]

Workers were well aware of the inherent difficulties in winning concessions from employers where the workforce was divided on ethnic lines.

The fact is that the people do realise what power they have got in themselves—even up there in Arandis (*the township set aside for Damara workers and their families*). . . . But the one thing which according to me isn't good is that they (*the workers in the compounds, particularly Ovambo contract workers*) just see them as an ethnic group. That isn't good. They just refer to them as 'Damaras' and that isn't very good, that's hurting. They have got that feeling that when they stand together they can achieve something, but the mood in which they want to achieve it, that's not very good. But they have got that realisation that if they stand in solidarity they can achieve something.

The only thing is to see a struggle like that one at Arandis as not particularly for the Arandis people but that all of us are being affected by it . . . the other people have to co-operate with the people of Arandis to show that they are not going to be used, like now they are being used.[14]

The disastrous potential of 'divide and rule' tactics had been amply demonstrated at Rössing eighteen months earlier in July 1975 when police, assisted by special South African mobile army units from the nearby Walvis Bay military base, were rushed to the Rössing complex when fighting broke out between Ovambos and a group of Xhosa construction workers imported from South Africa to work on the development of the huge mining project. 15 people were seriously injured, while others fled from the mine to avoid the confrontation. Full-scale violence reportedly developed after one or more people had lost their lives in clashes between rival groups of workers. According to a white worker at the mine, the Xhosa workers had been taunting the Ovambos and making derisive remarks, while the Ovambos maintained that the Xhosas had been brought into Namibia to "take the bread from their mouths".[15] Whatever the immediate reasons, the clash had its roots in the accentuation of ethnic differences under apartheid policies. In a statement issued in Walvis Bay, furthermore, the SWAPO branch secretary, Mr. Festus Naholo, accused mine officials at Rössing of failing to inform the police as soon as the threat of a clash became apparent. Why, Mr. Naholo asked, did the police arrive after the fight was almost over?—while in contrast, whenever there was a labour strike or demonstration, the police were at the scene immediately.[16]

The closing months of 1976 in fact saw a countrywide outburst of resistance to South African rule inside Namibia, particularly on the part of black students and teachers. The authorities' response revealed the state's continuing commitment to apartheid policies—despite its claim through the Turnhalle constitutional talks in progress at this time, that the Namibian people would decide their own future. From the beginning of November 1976, black students at schools throughout Namibia boycotted examinations and organised protests and demonstrations against the extension of South Africa's policy of 'Bantu education' to the territory. Leaflets were circulated attacking Bantu education as "the instrument of the homelands policy" while the Namibian Black Students Organization denounced it in a statement as "a propaganda machinery of apartheid dehumanization and discrimination". The police reacted with characteristic heavyhandedness to what amounted to a striking display of solidarity with students and young people in South Africa. At one school in Damaraland for example, children carrying placards commemorating the victims of the Soweto disturbances a few months before were baton-charged by police, backed up by troops in armoured cars.[17] Despite the arrest and detention of many students, some of whom are known to have been assaulted and given electric shock torture by the police, protests continued into 1977.[18]

Meanwhile, 237 Nama teachers were sacked from their jobs by the Department of Coloured, Rehoboth and Nama Affairs for disobeying a departmental order to return to work. Their defiance of apartheid education policies developed into "one of the bitterest and certainly the longest of disputes in recent southern African labour history".[19] It also revealed the tactics of the South African authorities, who worked through their tribal nominees in the Nama 'homeland' to weaken and intimidate the strikers.

Nama teachers throughout the country opted to go on strike on 9 November 1976 in a demand for salaries in line with those paid to Coloured teachers, and the building of more high schools for Namas, particularly one in an urban area. (Most Namas live in Windhoek and southern Namibia, where they have been allocated a 'homeland' in a remote rural region under the Odendaal plan. It has been official South African policy not to build any high schools outside the 'homelands' and in 1976 Namas were informed that the senior classes of one of their two existing secondary schools were to be closed down and replaced by a new high school in the reserve).[20] Although Namas are grouped with Coloureds under South Africa's racial classification scheme, Nama teachers have been paid at the lower 'Bantu' rate, are ineligible for the fringe benefits accruing to Coloured teachers, and as a result of inferior training facilities, tend to possess only 'Bantu' teaching qualifications.

Despite representations from the South West Africa Nama Teachers Association, the Minister of Coloured, Rehoboth and Nama Affairs, Mr. Hennie Smit, refused to meet the striking teachers to discuss their grievances. On 9 December, all those still on strike were informed that because of 'misconduct' their services were no longer required.[21] The teachers nevertheless remained on strike throughout the Christmas period and well into January 1977 in the face, according to the Teachers' Association, of 'strong propaganda' on the part of the Department of Coloured, Rehoboth and Nama Affairs, the South African-sponsored Nama Council (or tribal authority), and Nama delegates to the Turnhalle constitutional talks. Captain Hendrik Witbooi, the traditional Chief of the Witbooi section of the Namas and a prominent member of SWAPO, came under particular pressure. Captain Witbooi, the principal of a Nama school in Gibeon, was one of the striking teachers to be sacked by the authorities. He was subsequently informed that a new head teacher had been appointed in his place and warned that if he did not comply with South African government policy for the development of the Nama 'homeland' and the setting up of tribal authorities his position as Captain and accompanying monthly salary would be terminated.[22]

On 23 January, in the face of continuing threats and intransigence on the part of the South African government, the Teachers' Association decided to call off the strike. Nama teachers interviewed on 16 January, during the height of the dispute, made it clear that they totally rejected the state educational apparatus, and saw the way forward through private 'alternative' schools, built with voluntary contributions and open to children of all races.

> We feel that the only way out now, as we reject the Government and as we reject this particular department is to start really this what we call private schools. You see in that we feel that we will completely break away from the Government. . . .

> . . . we don't want those high schools only in so-called homelands, but in towns and cities where we can get teachers of other races . . . we are not talking only in terms of Namas. It should be in the cities and towns where all the peoples of also other ethnic groups can go to that school.[23]

Increasingly, as South Africa has stepped up its efforts to entrench an 'ethnic' framework of government in Namibia, action by black workers has taken the form of resistance to the apartheid system as a whole. Workers are not only concerned about their wages or conditions of employment. In the middle of 1977, for example, about 30 people working for the Bantu Commission Office and the Government Water Project in Omaruru, Ovamboland, went on strike in protest against intimidation aimed at gaining their support for tribal leaders.[24] Incidents of this kind reveal the deep-rooted desire for national unity and for freedom from the divisive policies of apartheid that exists among the black workforce—and indeed in Namibia as a whole. As will be shown in more detail in the following chapter, these are aspirations which have been most effectively articulated by the national liberation movement, SWAPO.

The rejection of tribal policies has inevitably provoked an increasingly violent response on the part of the authorities. In the opening months of 1978, grievances and tensions arising out of South African government policies culminated in a series of violent clashes in the black township of Katutura and disturbances in many other parts of Namibia. Over the period 28 February to 8 March in particular, at least 14 people were killed and many seriously injured in fierce street battles in Katutura between rival supporters of SWAPO (including many Ovambo contract workers) and the Democratic Turnhalle Alliance. The President of the Democratic Turnhalle Alliance at this time was Chief Clemens Kapuuo, the leader of the Herero delegation to the Turnhalle constitutional talks, and the DTA comprised substantial numbers of his Herero supporters. On 27 March, Chief Kapuuo himself was shot dead outside his shop in Katutura by two unknown assassins. All these events were immediately blamed by the South African authorities on SWAPO, and they took the Chief's death in particular as a cue for arresting large numbers of SWAPO members and national officials throughout Namibia, and for introducing sweeping new emergency powers of detention.[25]

In reality, there is ample evidence to support SWAPO's allegation that the South African government, by taking a partisan attitude to the tensions that were building up and, in particular, by sanctioning the distribution of firearms to DTA supporters, were themselves responsible for provoking the violence.

It is also clear that the clashes were aggravated by grievances arising out of the contract labour system and the economic situation in the country as a whole. At the height of the disturbances, and in the face of considerable provocation, contract workers in Katutura took disciplined and responsible action in an attempt to force the authorities to intervene decisively.

The background to the troubles was one of rising unemployment among black workers in the Windhoek area. The SWA Administrator General's decision, in October 1977, to abolish aspects of the pass laws and influx control (*see Ch. III*) meant that black workers from the reserves were now able to migrate to Windhoek and other white urban centres in search of jobs much more readily than in the past. Black unemployment, always an endemic feature of the apartheid economy, had in any case increased sharply in response to the development of the armed struggle in the north of the country and falling business confidence in Namibia's future. Black workers were being retrenched in both the agricultural and commercial sectors.[26] Windhoek's Town Clerk, Mr. Attie Arnold, revealed at the end of January that unemployment among established black Windhoek residents had recently risen to 12% and now affected about 1,600 people[27] quite apart from those arriving daily from the reserves in search of work.

Weeks before the disturbances erupted, the Windhoek municipal authorities were predicting clashes between rival groups of work-seekers. Their response, and that of many employers, seemed calculated to turn such forecasts into reality. In January, the *Windhoek Advertiser*, Namibia's main English-language newspaper, featured a picture of long queues at Windhoek's Employment Bureau, captioned by the remark that "every arrival of what looks like an employer is surrounded by dozens of men". A "rather prominent employer" interviewed at the Bureau, however, dismissed the problem by remarking that "it was not an unusual phenomenon to see hundreds of people standing there at this time of year".[28] A spokesman for Ovambo workers in Katutura told the press that the only reply given to work-seekers in the private sector was "Go look for work at SWAPO".[29]

At the beginning of February 1978, Mr. Attie Arnold announced that the flow of jobless black people into Windhoek had forced the municipality to consider measures to protect its employees at the Ovambo contract workers' hostel in Katutura. He claimed that between 500 and 1,000 unemployed workers were staying illegally at the hostel and forecast a confrontation between the township's established black residents and the newcomers, who were mainly from Ovamboland. The hostel staff were duly issued with firearms for their own "protection". The Windhoek police, for their part, reported a rising crime rate, particularly incidents of petty theft and housebreaking.[30]

But far from taking positive steps to alleviate the hardships caused by unemployment, the authorities blamed them on the workers themselves. "Many of [Katutura's permanent black residents] have been replaced by Ovambos who are prepared to work for half their wages" accused Mr. Arnold.[31] In fact, as a

96

circular sent to local employers by the Swakopmund Municipality in February 1978 reveals, employers were probably taking advantage of the situation to reduce their wage bills. The circular, which warned of imminent food shortages, hardships and riots in the black townships, pointed out that there were already more than 1,000 unemployed black workers in Swakopmund. It exhorted employers to register all their workers, including casual workers, to report all vacancies, and at all costs to reduce the temptation to "cut costs by sacking workers and employing others at lower rates".[32]

The municipal authorities had been approached by the SWA Administrator General, Justice Steyn, to suggest ways to stem the flow of black job-seekers into urban areas in the wake of the abolition of influx control. On 1 March 1978, Justice Steyn announced the formation of a Committee on Labour which would, it was reported, "among other things examine ways to resolve the problem of unemployment". The Committee would be responsible for creating work opportunities in towns and cities, and in the reserves, in order to "encourage [black job-seekers] back to their own areas". It would work "in co-operation with the Ovambo Government" (representatives of which were to sit on the Committee) to "put effective practices into operation, which would be to the benefit of all population groups in South West Africa."[33] While these were not specified, it was clear that the Committee envisaged the solution to unemployment as lying within the economic development and consequent entrenchment of the tribal "homelands".

Meanwhile, tension in Katutura had finally erupted. On the night of 28 February, two Ovambo men (one of them a SWAPO member, Angula Hennock) were killed, and 41 people injured, in street clashes in Katutura. Both SWAPO and the DTA had been holding meetings in the area, and according to SWAPO sources, fighting was sparked off when a fake message, purporting to come from SWAPO and stating that the meeting was cancelled, was found in the DTA meeting-place.[34] DTA members thereupon attacked SWAPO supporters, beating Angula Hennock to death with an iron bar. Police used tear gas and, according to one SWAPO supporter at the scene, "turned the searchlights mounted on top of the riot-vans into the eyes of the SWAPO fighters", temporarily blinding them.[35]

According to the authorities, the clashes were "tribal" in origin. Mr. A. G. C. Yssel, the retiring Mayor of Windhoek, declared for example that there had been unprovoked fights over relatively trivial matters. He had nevertheless inspected the damage, and had discovered that "just about every panel in the building used for training of municipal police had been damaged"[36]—a far from trivial target. On 1 March the Town Clerk, Mr. Arnold, held discussions with the police, while the Management Committee of the Municipal Council voted funds for the setting up of an "industrial commando" which was to be responsible for the protection of municipal property as well as applying "traffic control and other relevant services during times of riot".[37]

There was another even more sinister side to the response of the police and municipal authorities. SWAPO supporters confronted by rival members of the Democratic Turnhalle Alliance found themselves facing men armed with guns— a situation which, given the strict laws governing the possession and ownership of firearms by black people, could only have arisen with official sanction. Over the weekend 4/5 March, 12 more deaths occurred after clashes had allegedly been sparked off by DTA supporters attacking a group of SWAPO workers waiting at a bus stop in Katutura. Those who lost their lives included the chief aide to Chief Kapuuo, a former policeman who like the other members of the chief's large personal bodyguard was armed and defended himself with a shotgun. SWAPO workers interviewed by the *Windhoek Advertiser* stated that reinforcements of DTA supporters had been brought into Windhoek by truck from the Herero reserve to take part in the fighting, at Chief Kapuuo's instigation and with covert assistance from the police. They said that SWAPO supporters living in the ethnically mixed single men's quarters in Katutura (as opposed to the municipal hostel for Ovambo contract workers) were unable to leave their lodgings, because if they did so, roving bands of Hereros from the DTA "would attack the place and set it on fire with their belongings".[38] By 6 March the disturbances had spread to other parts of Namibia, with three deaths at Oka-karara, after Herero workers had attacked Ovambo employees of the Department of Water Affairs.

(Official policy on the distribution of firearms to supporters of the Democratic Turnhalle Alliance became clear following Chief Kapuuo's assassination. A number of the Chief's Herero followers taking part in his funeral procession on 8 April were seen to be carrying machine guns. As the cortege moved out of Katutura on its way to join the main road to Okahandja where the burial was to take place, a number of Ovambo contract workers from the municipal hostel reportedly started to throw stones. The mourners retaliated with gunfire, killing four people and wounding 12. Asked to comment on the fact that Chief Kapuuo's followers were apparently in possession of R-3 automatic assault rifles, the Windhoek Divisional Commissioner of Police, Brig. Verster, admitted that "he was aware that Bantu Affairs, now the Dept. of Plural Relations, did hand firearms to a number of Hereros". The Windhoek CID further confirmed that .303 rifles had been issued "a long time ago" to the chief's supporters by the Department of Plural Relations, although it denied that any Africans outside the established army units were in possession of automatic weapons).[39]

At this point, contract workers in the Katutura municipal hostel, many, if not the majority, of whom were SWAPO supporters, decided to call a general strike in protest at the violence and to force the authorities to take effective action to defuse the tension. About 2,000 of the 4,158 Ovambo workers regist-ered at that time at the hostel stayed away from work over the two days 6/7 March, and several large industries and businesses in Windhoek reported that attendance was down to 40%.[40] Police were moved in to the main gates of the

Katutura hostel, and tear gas was used against groups of workers who had been trying to persuade others to join the strike.[41]

The strikers' demands, as communicated to Justice Steyn when he visited the hostel to address the workers on 7 March, were a clear appeal for reason. They included the immediate return to their homes of those Hereros who had been brought into Katutura to take part in the fighting, the immediate release of hostel residents who had been arrested for carrying "dangerous weapons" (i.e. knives, clubs and sticks—one of the main complaints was that DTA supporters armed with guns were immune from prosecution); the state hospital, which had allegedly been refusing treatment to hostel residents, to admit everyone injured in the unrest without discrimination; all those responsible for the killings to be arrested and brought before the courts; and an assurance that none of the strikers would be dismissed from their jobs.[42] The *Windhoek Advertiser* commented that it was "significant that strikers had no complaints about salary or even working conditions, but merely stayed in the compound because they felt "it would cause less bloodshed".[43]

The strikers returned to work following Justice Steyn's visit to the hostel. Meanwhile, SWAPO joined with other political parties, including the DTA, and representatives of the churches, the police and the security police, in the formation of a committee to prevent the recurrence of further violence.[44] In addition, it urged the South African government to appoint a "sincere and honest judicial commission of inquiry" to establish the real causes of the disturbances which had, over a period of four weeks, led to the deaths of at least 26 people.[45] The Committee on Labour appointed earlier in the year by Justice Steyn nevertheless announced at a press conference that it had "established beyond doubt that the trouble in Katutura recently had been politically inspired and that SWAPO was solely responsible."[46]

Meanwhile, attacks on SWAPO supporters continued, while the most obvious response of the authorities was to move police reinforcements into Windhoek from South Africa and, from the beginning of April, to bring the activities of SWAPO inside Namibia to a standstill by arresting and detaining virtually the entire leadership and many prominent members. Those picked up in the course of this countrywide purge included Mr. Leonard Nghigepandulwa, the chairman of the Union of Namibian Workers in the Katutura contract workers' hostel. (The National Union of Namibian Workers, whose formation under SWAPO's, leadership is described in the following chapter, had played a leading role in organising the hostel residents to combat the violence of early March). Five years before Mr. Nghigepandulwa had been the No. 12 accused in the trial of alleged leaders of the 1971/72 contract workers' strike.[47]

These events formed part of what, with hindsight, can only be interpreted as a concerted campaign by South Africa to undermine and if necessary to eliminate SWAPO as a contender for the government of an independent Namibia. In the eyes of the South African government, collective action by black workers of the kind that had confronted Justice Steyn on his visit to the Katutura hostel, constituted an integral part of popular resistance to their apartheid policies. It must therefore be suppressed along with SWAPO's other activities. The strategy culminated in South Africa' decision, announced at the end of September 1978, to reject the UN Secretary General's proposals for a negotiated transition to independence, and to press ahead unilaterally with 'elections' which as expected, brought the Democratic Turnhalle Alliance to power in Namibia.

# IX

# Unity is Strength

I want to tell our fellow-workers that the weak point we have [to remedy] in order to change the system is unity and co-operation. And we must not distinguish whether some workers are sleeping in a compound and some are staying in the single quarters and some in the so-called locations. All of us who are exploited, we blacks, we must know that we are all workers. We workers want to be in unity. We workers in Namibia, we want to unite. It don't matter what kind of work he is doing, each and every worker should come into that union. After such unity and co-operation have been established, it is only then that it will be possible to campaign for better working conditions, for higher wages and to embark on any other action which will change the working conditions.

Once workers have organised and united, they will be able to form a union, they will try to make other workers aware of the conditions in which they are working. In such a union of workers, we are going to teach one another how people should respect one another and regard themselves as human beings. We know that if a person is starving he will become wise, he will learn something from that starvation. Because we are quite aware that we are being oppressed here in Namibia. It is only through a union that we will be able to force the Government to change the conditions under which we are working, and it is only through the union that we will be able to make an end to the exploitation of man by man.

Because we know that we can only force the Government if we are united. We the workers of Namibia we have to unite—all the workers in the country have to unite, then we will be able to embark on the kind of action that will force the Government to attend to our problems. If we cannot unite then we will just continue to be exploited and oppressed.

*—Contract worker in Windhoek, 1977[1]*

The South West Africa People's Organization, SWAPO of Namibia, has been recognised by the United Nations General Assembly since 1973 as the national liberation movement and authentic representative of the Namibian people. In December 1976, UN recognition was made exclusive, and SWAPO was given full observer status at the General Assembly and participation rights in all UN agencies. While this position has never been fully accepted by, among others, the British government, it cannot be denied that SWAPO has since its earliest days addressed itself to the issues of most immediate and pressing concern to the

Namibian people—freedom from poverty and exploitation, self-determination and national unity, and the right to live unmolested with their families in the place of their choice. SWAPO in fact has its roots deep in the contract labour system which forms the economic core of apartheid in Namibia.

According to Mr. Vorster, the South African Prime Minister until September 1978:

> SWAPO was conceived and born in sin . . . it was born in Cape Town, as the child of four communists. . . . At its birth its name was the Ovamboland People's Organization, or the OPO. These four communists made Sam Nujoma, who is an Ovambo, the leader of this organization. In 1958 they realised that it was a mistake to call it the Ovamboland People's Organization and, as such, to send it out into the world. They then changed its name to the South West Africa People's Organization. That is where the name SWAPO comes from.[2]

The people of Namibia themselves have a different version of events. Vinnia Ndadi, a former contract worker, recalled meeting an old friend, in June 1959. This friend had told him that "We have a political party for Africans now, set up by Ovambo workers who'd been to Cape Town. Many of us are joining the party and everybody's talking about it. It's called the OPO. . . . They hold public meetings, recruit members and try to organise the people into OPO local branches. . . . They're saying, 'We don't want contract labour anymore. The OPO will fight the South African government and its rotten contract system'."[3]

The Ovamboland People's Organization, OPO, had been formed in 1957 among a group of Namibian students and contract workers in Cape Town, South Africa, under the leadership of Herman Toivo ja Toivo.[4] Born in 1924, Herman ja Toivo had travelled abroad while serving with the South African forces during the Second World War, but in 1957 was working as a shop assistant in a white-owned grocery business in a Cape Town suburb. He made contact with other Namibians, and established a centre for meetings and discussions in a barber's shop. It was out of these that OPO developed.[5]

Herman ja Toivo was deported from Cape Town in 1958 for sending a taped message to the United Nations outlining South African oppression of his people. Returning to Namibia as a regional organiser he launched the OPO in Windhoek and the north during the early months of 1959, with the help of others such as Sam Nujoma and Jacob Kahangua. "In little more than a year the OPO became a mass organization, its political strongholds and branch structure based solidly (though not exclusively) in the contract workers' compounds of the towns and mines."[6] This was a period of mounting resistance to apartheid and violent responses on the part of the police and South African authorities. In January 1959, fishery workers at a canning factory in Walvis Bay organised a go-slow strike in protest at the behaviour of a white foreman. Meanwhile in Windhoek, black residents of the old location who faced forcible removal to the new township of Katutura were mounting boycotts of the bus

102

service, the municipal beer-halls and the cinema. On 10 December 1959, South African police killed 13 people and wounded 52 others when they opened fire on a crowd of residents manning a picket line. "In the clearest possible terms the South African occupation regime had shown that it would ruthlessly crush all attempts at peaceful persuasion and popular mobilisation."[7]

In 1960, conscious of the fact that the contract labour system was but one, though a crucial, aspect of South Africa's occupation of Namibia, and of the need for a fully national resistance movement, the OPO was renamed the South West Africa People's Organization, SWAPO. From its earliest beginnings Namibia's national liberation movement was thus closely linked to the aspirations of workers and their grievances. The name it first chose, Ovamboland People's Organization, indicated that the great majority of contract workers, the most oppressed part of the labour force, came from Ovamboland. (In practice, contract workers are often referred to by employers as "Ovambos", whether they actually come from Ovamboland or not). While the South African government has energetically promoted the idea that SWAPO is a "tribal" movement, and the vehicle for Ovambo domination of the rest of the Namibian people, its history shows that it is first and foremost an organization of Namibians as workers, and not as members of tribes or ethnic groups. SWAPO today is comprised of Namibians of all races and from all parts of the country. (South African propaganda has in recent years taken a substantial battering as a number of political parties and groups of Namibians based in the south of the country have disbanded and joined SWAPO).

Vinnia Ndadi recalls his first meeting with Sam Nujoma, who had come to address workers in Walvis Bay. Sam Nujoma introduced himself, and then gave the background of his organization:

> We started in Cape Town, but now we are trying to bring all the people of South West Africa together in OPO. . . . We all know, especially you contract workers, that we've suffered much under this system. Our people have been forced to work for slave wages under miserable conditions—dictated by these racist Boers. Families are broken up and we're made to live in lousy compounds like this. Not treated like human beings, but like cattle. One day we'll bring an end to this system, however, and we'll work as free men, each and every one choosing his work according to his desire and needs, without force.

Vinnia Ndadi remembers: "Then he asked us, 'Will you join the struggle to abolish contract labour?' Everyone shouted, 'Yes! Yes! That's what we want!' "[8]

By the end of 1959, the Walvis Bay branch of the OPO had a membership of several thousand people.[9]

Vinnia Ndadi himself became an OPO organiser, and later a leader of SWAPO. He describes a meeting in Ovamboland, held to explain the change from OPO to SWAPO. He told the members that "OPO was a regional organization, formed by Ovambo workers in Cape Town and was a workers' union against contract labour. SWAPO's main objective, on the other hand, was to help liberate all the peoples of South West Africa from Boer oppression and win national independence."[10] Members of the Special Branch who had attended many of his meetings later arrested Vinnia Ndadi. He was held incommunicado and in solitary confinement by the police for three months. An African constable wondered why he was being kept in isolation: " 'Are you a SWAPO man?' he asked. I looked at him. 'Yes, I am.' ' I see. So you're involved in politics. Now I know why.' "[11] During interrogation the prisoner was confronted with evidence that he had been working for SWAPO which was not, and is not today, an illegal organization. A Special Branch Officer told him: "We'll show you that what you're attempting can't succeed. It'll just bring you misery—and everyone else involved too. You have a real problem, *Kaffir!!*"[12]

Although SWAPO has never been outlawed by the South African government (unlike the liberation movements of South Africa itself), its members and supporters have suffered persecution and harassment at the hands of the authorities and employers alike. From its early days mobilisation had to be carried out discreetly. One black Namibian, Thomas, for example, revealed that he had been banned from teaching because of his SWAPO activities, and that he could not find a job for the same reason. "They announced on the radio that those who are banned from a job because of politics are not allowed to get another job" he said. He lost other jobs, which he had obtained only through producing forged papers showing a different name, when it was discovered that he had been politically active in Windhoek. At his last job with a bantustan authority he was recognised and questioned. Why had he left his last employment? He replied, "They said I am a politician". Back came the answer: "So you are not allowed to do any job in this department either if you are a politician. Go to your office, take everything that belongs to you, and leave. I don't care where to. Don't ask me for money". He had lost a whole month's salary.[13]

Hans and two of his friends said that if someone was known to belong to SWAPO he was blacklisted by the employment authorities.[14] Another commentator, this time a white personnel officer on a Namibian mine, has also described this practice:

> The permanent trump card in the Labor (sic) Officer's hand of informal rules is his "blacklist", a list which he keeps of all workers who are or might be "agitators" and "troublemakers" at home or more especially in the Police Zone. Such "listed" people simply find that there is no work availabe for them. . . . As far as I could determine, the criteria for placement on the list are purely arbitrary. Many people are placed on the list on the basis of information received from the South African security police. Others are placed on the list by the Labor Officer on the basis of complaints he has had from white employers. Apparently, there is no impartial investigation into the alleged misbehaviour, and it certainly is difficult for the black-listed worker to appeal his listing as the Labor Officer can simply deny the

existence of the "black-list" and claim there was no "suitable" employment. Instead, black listed workers have to use different strategies like changing "identities" in obtaining employment.[15]

The same observer remarks that "any clerk or worker who tries to bypass or undercut the chief clerk is relatively easily framed by a whisper or two from him of 'agitator' or 'SWAPO' in the Compound Manager's ear".[16]

Many black workers who are SWAPO supporters are afraid to say so publicly for fear of harassment. Workers at the Oamites mine, for example, were reported by a visitor to Namibia in November 1977 to have been sacked from their jobs for their SWAPO sympathies.[17] At the Consolidated Diamond Mines compound, the company has acquired a more tolerant reputation—SWAPO branches are in theory permitted to operate openly and are allowed to hold a public meeting at each hostel once in every four months.[18] Other recent visitors to CDM, however, have reported that any worker engaging in political activity was quickly dismissed—a practice which was confirmed by a former senior CDM employee.[19]

In August 1978—in one of the very rare instances of this kind of harassment reaching the press and media—it was reported that the son of the leader of the Coloured Labour Party in Namibia had been sacked from his position at a Windhoek insurance company because he had openly associated with SWAPO. Mr. Andy Kloppers had relinquished his position as Chairman of the Labour Party Youth League to join SWAPO.[20]

Since its early beginnings in OPO, SWAPO has grown into a genuinely national resistance movement, mobilising Namibians of all ages, from all parts of the country and all occupation groups. Since 1966, SWAPO guerilla fighters have been actively engaged in an armed struggle against South African forces, while as the war has developed, the movement has taken on other responsibilities —such as caring for the many thousands of Namibian refugees who have crossed the borders into neighbouring Angola, Zambia and Botswana. In 1968 Herman ja Toivo, SWAPO's most eminent founder member, was sentenced to 20 years imprisonment under South Africa's Terrorism Act, and incarcerated on Robben Island along with 36 other SWAPO members convicted at the same trial.

While the struggle against apartheid has taken on new forms, contract workers have remained SWAPO's "most consistent and militant base".[21] It is this which perhaps most clearly distinguishes SWAPO from the many other political parties and groupings which exist in Namibia. Commentators on the 1971/72 general strike have recognised that without SWAPO's national organisation and branch structure, such widespread and effective mass industrial activity would hardly have been possible.[22] More recently, the need for a separate trade union organisation, sharing SWAPO's aims and ideals and closely linked to the wider struggle for national liberation, has been recognised in the formation of the National Union of Namibian Workers (NUNW), also referred to as the Namibian Workers' Union, (NAWU).

During 1977, groups of workers in Namibia began to meet to discuss and plan the formation of a general trade union for all Namibian workers, with

different industrial sections and with branches at each major work-centre.[23]  A
visitor to Namibia in the first half of that year reported that the proposed union,
while open to all, was initially being organized among contract workers in the
mines and factories.  It had already set up literacy courses in the Katutura
municipal compound where it held regular meetings.[24]  One such meeting was
described a few months later by a Swedish journalist on a visit to southern
Africa:

> One evening I participated in a trade union meeting in a church in Wind-
> hoek where I had been invited by Pastor Max who works among immigrant
> labourers from Ovamboland.  There were 25 people in the church.  They
> discussed proposals for a constitution for forming a trade union. . . .
>
> That evening in the church was a historical event, since there have not
> been any trade unions in Namibia up until now.  Those participating there
> asked me as a representative of a Swedish newspaper about the situation
> in Namibia.  The meeting started at 7 p.m. and ended at 10.30 p.m.  Then
> the chairman said: 'We must finish now otherwise we may risk an encounter
> with the police'.[25]

According to SWAPO's representative in London, trade union organization
among workers in Namibia at the beginning of 1978 was already widespread at
plant or factory level, but the work of co-ordinating the various local groups,
which was being organized by SWAPO, had not yet been completed.[26]  This
goal of "unity and solidarity among all workers in Namibia" has been written
into the constitution of the National Union of Namibian Workers. (The *Draft
Constitution* of the NAWU is reproduced in full in Appendix A).  It is a goal
which the South African government, through its enforcement of apartheid in
Namibia, has consistently endeavoured to defeat.

Nevertheless, the critical role of Namibia's workers in the political processes
which must ultimately lead to true independence was again demonstrated towards the end of 1978. In June 1978, the South African administration in Namibia started to register potential voters for elections intended—as was clear to
many at the time and is now obvious in retrospect — to install the tribally-
based Democratic Turnhalle Alliance as South Africa's own choice of "independent" government in Namibia. The elections were duly held in December 1978,
in defiance of the United Nations and as a direct rebuttal of more than a year and
a half of negotiations with the five Western members of the Security Council.
Throughout the proceedings, action in the work-place formed a key element of
popular resistance to South Africa's plans, in the face of widespread harassment
and intimidation. The response of the authorities was swift; SWAPO members
who distributed pamphlets in Grooftontein and Walvis Bay calling on workers
to go on strike to disrupt voters' registration were declared to be "traitors" by
the SWA Administrator General, Justice Steyn (*see Ch. VI*). A few months later,
in November, the Divisional Inspector of Labour in Namibia announced that
black people who took part in strikes would not, as in the past, simply be sent
back to their areas of origin, but would be charged and tried for illegal action.

106

Strikes were only legal, the statement continued, if they complied with the terms of Wages and Industrial Conciliation Amendment Proclamation of 1978 (*see Ch. VI*). Otherwise they were criminal acts.[27]   The Inspector's warning was clearly in response to calls by SWAPO for a boycott of the impending elections. White employers, for their part, cooperated closely with the South African administration and the police in ensuring that their employees were brought to the polling booths (*see Appendix B*).

While a trade union structure affiliated to SWAPO was beginning to take shape in 1978, the liberation movement itself remains the chief organization representing the interests of Namibian workers. When SWAPO members and officials inside Namibia are harassed for their opposition to South African policies, the effects of the victimisation are felt by black workers. To drive people to the South African stage-managed elections of December 1978, for example, teachers and nurses were told that those who did not vote would be regarded as SWAPO supporters, and "will have to look for work with SWAPO".[28]

Despite Pretoria's manoeuvres to establish a proxy government in Namibia led by the Democratic Turnhalle Alliance, which would enable South Africa to retain effective control of the territory while granting the semblance of independence, there is a deep conviction among the majority of the people that true freedom will come. To most Namibians, this means that their country will be led by SWAPO. Even some of the multinational companies operating in Namibia seem to have accepted the likelihood of such an outcome. While the South African authorities were preparing for the December 1978 elections, Mr. Harry Oppenheimer, head of the Anglo-American Corporation, the parent company of Consolidated Diamond Mines, was holding talks with SWAPO to discover what sort of economic policy a future independent government might follow. He learned that SWAPO was thinking of taking at least a 70% share of the diamond industry "for the people", while in the strategically important uranium mining sector, an 80% share was envisaged. But in the final analysis, Mr. Oppenheimer was told, "the people will decide", through negotiations between an independent Namibian government and Anglo American and other companies concerned.[29]

There is no doubt that SWAPO's plans and policies imply a new deal for black workers, who with their families make up the vast majority of the Namibian people. The history of the liberation movement in Namibia cannot be separated from the struggle of working people for improved wages and working conditions, and for their political rights. SWAPO's roots in Namibia's labour force mean that the destiny of the country must ultimately hinge on its workers.

*Namibians taken prisoner by German troops during the early colonial period*

Photo: KZA

Excavations at the Tsumeb mine in 1900

Photo: KZA

Searching for diamonds near Luderitz 1908

*Housing for a Coloured worker's family near Luderitz*　　　　　*Photo: Peter Fraenkel*

*Accommodation for African farmworkers*

*Advertisements from commercial magazines in Namibia*

*Mineworker at the Tsumeb copper mine*　　　　　　　　　*Photo: Ingelore Frank*

*Workers' accommodation at the Rössing Uranium mine*　　　　　*Photo: SWAPO*

*Advertisement in a Windhoek newspaper*

*Mr. Harry Oppenheimer, the head of the Anglo–American Corporation, in his private helicopter*

Brushes and shovels are used to expose the diamonds at the Oranjemund workings
Photo: Gavin Shreeve

Aerial view of the Consolidated Diamond Mines complex at Oranjemund
Photo: United Nations/A. Reininger

*Tractors and earth moving equipment at CDM*  *Photo: United Nations/A. Reininger*

*Workers at CDM*  *Photo: United Nations/A. Reininger*

*Railway workers near Otjiwarongo*                    Photo: *Jurgen Muller-Schneck*

*Dockers at Walvis Bay*

*Raw copper awaiting shipment at Walvis Bay*

Photo: Kimmo Kiljunen

*Entrance to the new contract workers' hostel in Katutura*          *Photo: Kimmo Kiljunen*

*The contract workers' compound at the Tsumeb mine*

*Black workers on strike in the Katutura compound, December* 1971

*SWAPO supporters in Windhoek*                    *Photo: SWAPO*

*Workers in Windhoek, December 1978*             *Photo: SWAPO*

*Election meeting of the Democratic Turnhalle Alliance, December* 1978        *Photo: SWAPO*

*Police at a SWAPO rally, December* 1978        *Photo: SWAPO*

*John Ya Otto, SWAPO Secretary for Labour, addressing the International Labour Organisation, June 1978*                                                                    *Photo: SWAPO*

*SWAPO supporters in Windhoek, December 1978*                                        *Photo: SWAPO*

*Cannery workers on the beach at Walvis Bay*

*Photo: United Nations/A. Reininger*

# References

The following abbreviations are used:

| | |
|---|---|
| BBC | British Broadcasting Corporation Monitoring Service |
| CT | Cape Times, Cape Town |
| Debates | South African House of Assembly Debates (Hansard) |
| FOCUS | FOCUS on Political Repression in Southern Africa, IDAF news bulletin |
| FM | Financial Mail, Johannesburg |
| FT | Financial Times, London |
| GN | Guardian, London |
| MS | Morning Star, London |
| Obs | Observer, London |
| RDM | Rand Daily Mail, Johannesburg |
| SALB | South African Labour Bulletin, Durban |
| Star | Star Weekly Airmail edition, Johannesburg |
| T | The Times, London |
| Tel | Daily Telegraph, London |
| WA | Windhoek Advertiser, Windhoek |
| WO | Windhoek Observer, Windhoek |

## I. INTRODUCTION

1. *SALB*, Vol. 4, Nos. 1 and 2. January–February 1978, p. 44.
2. United Nations Council for Namibia, *Decree No. 1 for the Protection of the Natural Resources of Namibia*, enacted 27 September 1974; UN General Assembly Resolution 3295 (*XXIX*) of 1974.
3. The British Parliamentary Select Committee was set up after the *Guardian* newspaper in London had published details about the wages and conditions of black workers in both South Africa and Namibia. In 1974 Lord Brockway pressed the British government to set up a similar inquiry into conditions in Namibia. He was told that the Select Committee on South Africa had "the competence" to act in this matter. Lord Brockway then pointed out that the Committee had taken the view "that Namibia was outside its terms of reference, as the United Nations had declared it to be an independent country". The government reply, delivered by Lord Goronwy Roberts, was: "On the question of whether Namibia was ruled out by the Select Committee that may be so. But there is nothing to prevent them from ruling it back into their consideration". This however, the Committee chose not to do.
4. United Nations Department of Political Affairs, Trusteeship and Decolonization, *Decolonization* No. 9/Revised edition, December 1977, *Issue on Namibia*, p. 5.
5. Robert L. Bradford, *The Blacks to the Wall: The Condition of the Africans in the Mandated Territory of South West Africa*, International Conference on Namibia, Oxford, 23–26 March, 1966, p. 3.
6. ibid, p. 3.
7. ibid, pp. 3–4.
8. Namibia's permanent white population, comprising an estimated 20,000 German-speaking people, 15,000 English and Portuguese-speakers and 55,000 Afri-kaans-speakers, is in fact just as culturally diverse as the "Coloured" or "African" groupings. Putting the whites into a single category, however, means that they together comprise the second largest "population group" in Namibia, after the Ovambos. (In addition to permanent residents, the white population includes an estimated 15,000 people domiciled in South Africa. Many of these are civil servants employed in the SWA Administration). (Wolfgang H. Thomas, *Economic Deveopment in Namibia — Towards Acceptable Development Strategies for Independent Namibia*, Kaiser-Grunewald 1978, p. 20). Namas (some of the earliest inhabitants of Namibia), Rehoboth Basters (a mixed race group who migrated to Namibia from South Africa in the 19th century) and Coloureds (also mixed race) are all classified as "Coloured" for administrative purposes. (The South African government has nevertheless been extremely ambivalent about the Namas, and has from time to time returned them to the "African" category). The African or "Bantu" group is comprised of Ovambos, Kavangos, Caprivians, Hereros, Damaras, Kaokolanders, Tswanas and Bushmen (see pp. 18–21 and table on p. 11).
9. This was the recommendation of the Odendaal "Commission of Enquiry into South West African Affairs", set up by the South African government in 1962 in the face of mounting international criticism of the way it was administering Namibia. It reported two years later. Its proposals for setting up bantustans in Namibia were substantially accepted by South Africa even though the Commission pointed out that at least six of the designated "homelands" were economically unviable. The Commission also set out a detailed plan for extending Namibia's economic infrastructure, particularly com-

munications and a hydro-electric scheme, which were to benefit, most of all, the white community and overseas investors. (*See Chapter II*).

10. Resolution 2145 (*XXI*) was adopted by 114 votes to two (Portugal and South Africa), with three abstentions (France, Malawi and the United Kingdom). By resolution 2372 *XXII*) adopted in June 1968, the General Assembly renamed South West Africa "Namibia".

11. Resolution 264 (1969).

12. The Court declared: (a) that the continued presence of South Africa was illegal and that therefore South Africa was under obligation to withdraw its administration from Namibia, immediately; (b) that States Members of the United Nations were under obligation to recognize the illegality of South Africa's presence in Namibia and the invalidity of its acts on behalf of or concerning Namibia and to refrain from any acts or dealings with the Government of South Africa implying recognition of the legality of such presence and administration; and (c) that it was incumbent on States not Members of the United Nations to co-operate in the action taken by the United Nations with regard to Namibia. (*International Court of Justice Reports* 1971). Five years previously, in July 1966, the International Court had failed to deliver a judgement on the Namibian issue, declaring that it had no power to decide the dispute.

13. Statement delivered at a press conference in Lusaka, 22 September, 1978; reprinted in *Zimbabwe People's Voice* 30.9.78.

## II. THE APARTHEID ECONOMY

1. Africa Bureau *Fact Sheet No.* 51 May/ June, 1977. Under the *South West Africa Affairs Act* of 1969, control over some two-thirds of Namibia's budget was transferred to Pretoria from Windhoek. (This Act, which marked a milestone in South Africa's efforts to enforce apartheid in Namibia, in fact removed legislative and administrative responsibility for a total of 25 broad categories of subject including labour relations, income and taxes, mining and minerals, registration of birth, deaths and marriages, and censorship, from the South West Africa *Legislative Assembly* to the South African parliament). *GN* 14.8.78.

2. United Nations General Assembly, *Report of the Special Committee on the situation with regard to the implementation of the declaration on the granting of independence to colonial countries and peoples (hereafter Decolonization Committee Report), Ch. V,* 24 October, 1975, Appendix II.

3. W. H. Thomas, *Economic Development in Namibia—Towards Acceptable Development Strategies for Independent Namibia,* Kaiser Grünewald 1978, p. 30

4. United Nations Office of Public Information. *Objective: Justice* Vol. 8, No. 3. Autumn 1976 p. 30.

5. Roger Murray et al. *The Role of Foreign Firms in Namibia,* Study Project on External Investment in South Africa and Namibia (South West Africa). Africa Publications Trust 1974 p. 89 ff.

6. *Report of the United Nations Council for Namibia,* Vol. 1 1976, p. 26; Letter from Peter Katjavivi, SWAPO's representative in UK and Western Europe, *T* 4.4.75.

7. Renfrew Christie. *The Political Economy of the Kunene River Schemes.* M.A. thesis, University of Cape Town, South Africa, 1975 p. 98.

8. Roger Murray et al, op. cit. pp. 109–110.

9. De Beers Consolidated Mines Ltd., *Annual Report* 1976, p. 6.

10. W. H. Thomas, *The Economy of South West Africa: An Overall Perspective,* paper presented to the 1975 Summer School of the Centre for Extra-Mural Studies of the University of Cape Town, South Africa, p. 20—see also below Chapters IV and V.

11. *Obs.* 17.11.74.

12. Africa Bureau *Fact Sheet No.* 51 May June 1977.
In October 1978, South Africa's Prime Minister Mr. P. W. Botha told journalists that Namibia had made "substantial progress" under South Africa's guidance. South Africa's support was not only a matter of money, he said, but embraced railways, harbours, postal and telegraphic services, research in various directions, water and power supplies and general economic development under South African leadership. Between 1961 and 1977 the Republic had contributed R637 m. to Namibia's development in the form of special subsidies, loans for electrical supply and building main roads. This did not include about R200 m. spent yearly on peace-keeping forces "to maintain the security and peace in South West Africa against Marxist insurgency from outside". (*CT* 20.10.78).

13. *Report of the United Nations Council for Namibia.* Vol. 1 1976 p. 32.

14. ibid.

15. Murray et al op. cit. p. 51.

16. W. H. Thomas, *The Economy of South West Africa,* op. cit. p. 18.

17. For a detailed account of the steps taken by South Africa to implement the Odendaal proposals, up to and during the Turnhalle constitutional talks of 1975/76, see *All Options and None—The Constitutional Talks in Namibia,* IDAF Fact Paper No. 3, August 1976. Unlike those in South Africa itself, Namibia's tribal reserves have always been described as "homelands" rather than "bantustans" by the South African authorities for the

110

reason that two of the groups allocated to reserves by Odendaal—the Namas and the Rehoboth Basters—are in other respects officially classified as "Coloureds" rather than "Bantu" or "Natives", and are grouped with Namibia's Coloured (i.e. mixed race) population for administrative purposes.

18. United Nations Department of Political Affairs, Trusteeship and Decolonization: *Decolonization* No. 9/Revised Edition. December 1977, *Issue on Namibia*.

19. J. H. Wellington, *South West Africa and its Human Issues*, Oxford 1967, quoted in Peter Fraenkel, *The Namibians of South West Africa*, Minority Rights Group Report No. 19. New edition 1978.

20. Robert J. Gordon, *Mines, Masters and Migrants: Life in a Namibian Mine Compound*, Johannesburg 1977 p. 27.
The South African authorities have repeatedly pointed out that large sums have been allocated to developing water resources in Namibia. In a letter dated 27 May 1975 to the UN Secretary General, for example, the then South African Foreign Minister Dr. Hilgard Muller stressed that "a total of R139 million has so far been spent on 177 domestic water supply schemes constructed and operated by the State throughout the Territory. . . . I would like to add that my Government is at present giving active consideration to assisting the inhabitants with the further development of the water resources of the Territory at an estimated cost of some R333 million." (*Objective: Justice*, Vol. 7 No. 3, July–September 1975 p. 13). He was referring primarily to the Kunene water scheme on the border of Angola and Namibia, which was designed chiefly to supply water and electricity to the territory's mining and fishing industries. Water supply and irrigation plans for Ovamboland were in reality very much secondary considerations, and have not so far contributed markedly to the economic development of this area. As an authority on the economics of the Kunene scheme has pointed out, "Mining development has sent demand for electricity soaring and has threatened destructive competition with farmers for water. For separate development to succeed the Ovamboland pastoral economy needs bolstering by irrigated farming, so that labour may continue to be reproduced there, for 'Migrant' supply to the south. The Kunene schemes are designed to supply the south with all three commodities. . . ." (Renfrew Christie, *Who Benefits by the Kunene Hydro-Electric Schemes?* Social *Dynamics* 2(1) 31–43 1976, p. 34) Christie states, further on, "The ruling groups will benefit primarily and massively from the Kunene schemes. We have seen that the best agricultural, fishing and mining areas are allocated to Whites, and that the Kunene scheme will bring water and

power to these 'White' areas in great quantities, to facilitate their development. . . . It is possible that irrigated farming will succeed in Ovamboland on a large scale in due course, although this is by no means certain." (ibid p. 36). Further reports suggest that so far incipient irrigation attempts have failed, mainly due to bad relations between local populations and the white supervisory and technical personnel. (Christie, M.A. Thesis op. cit. p. 169).

21. Wellington, quoted in Fraenkel, op. cit.

22. UN *Decolonizaton Committee Report*, 15 September 1977, Ch. IV. Annex II.

23. Gordon op. cit. p. 222. SWANLA, the South West Africa Native Labour Association, was the sole recruiting agency for black labour until 1972.

24. South African Department of Foreign Affairs, *South West Africa Survey* 1974, p. 45. By 1973, however, the total amount of loans granted by the BIC was merely "in excess of R400,000", while a further R1 million was due to be loaned to "about 150 businessmen" up to 1976/7. (ibid).

25. John Kane-Berman, *Contract Labour in South West Africa*, South African Institute of Race Relations, Johannesburg 1972, appendix (iii) p xiii.

26. Murray et al, op. cit. p. 61.

27. Ruaha Voipio, *The Labour Situation in South West Africa*, South African Institute of Race Relations, Johannesburg 1973, p. 2.

28. Murray et al, op. cit. p. 63. The Rio Tinto–Zinc Corporation has a policy of employing local Damara workers from the nearby reserve at the Rössing uranium mine near Swakopmund. However it also employs Ovambo contract workers, and there are indications that the latter may be given some preference by the management in the wake of strike action by Damara employees at the end of 1976. (*See Ch. V p. 56 ff*).

29. UN *Decolonizaton Committee Report*, 29 September 1976. Ch. IV, Annex II.

30. Republic of South Africa, Department of Labour, *Manpower Survey* 1975, quoted in W. H. Thomas, *Economic Development in Namibia*, op. cit. Table 21 p. 196.

31. W. H. Thomas, *Economic Development in Namibia* op cit. Table 22 p. 197. The *South African Labour Bulletin*, in a recent study of Namibian labour, has also estimated that out of a population of approximately one million, over 150,000 people work for wages, of whom about 30,000 are whites. (*SALB* Vol. 4 Nos. 1 and 2. Jan–Feb. 1978).

32. See also Ch. III. At the end of 1977, through reforms initiated by the SWA Administrator General, Africans were permitted to purchase land in black townships.

33. *SALB*, Vol. 4 Nos. 1 and 2, Jan–Feb. 1978.

34. *Report of the United Nations Council for*

*Namibia*, Vol. 1, 1976, quoting official statistics.

35.  W. H. Thomas *Economic Development in Namibia* op. cit. p. 286 n. 39. John Kane-Berman, the chief chronicler of the contract workers' strike of 1971–72, has estimated that at the time of the strike, the labour force contained a total of 43,000 contract workers from Ovamboland, Kavangoland and Angola, distributed as follows:

| | |
|---|---|
| Farming | 10,900 |
| Domestic service | 2,700 |
| Mining | 12,800 |
| Fishing | 3,000 |
| Government, commerce and industry | 14,000 |

(John Kane-Berman, op cit. p. 4).

36.  Ovambos not only constitute the largest "population group" in Namibia (46.5%), but have also been driven to contract labour to a greater extent than others through population pressure and land hunger. As long ago as 1954 a white commissioner spoke about over-population: "As a result . . . more and more men have to leave the area to go out to work, not only to provide for their families, but in the case of those who want to buy land, to earn the high price of land." (Quoted in Gordon, op. cit. p. 30). One researcher has estimated that in 1959 about 38% of Ovambo men were away on contract work but that less than 10 years later this had risen to 67% (P. D. Banghart, *A Study of Migrant Labour in South West Africa*, M. A. Thesis, University of Stellenbosch, South Africa, quoted in Gordon op. cit. p. 220). In a more recent study the *South African Labour Bulletin* has estimated that between one third and one half of Ovambo men are working in the Police Zone at any one time. (Vol. 4 Nos. 1 and 2 Jan–Feb. 1978). The great majority of Ovambo men undoubtedly spend the bulk of their first 30 years of adult life away from their homes and families on contract. According to a white personnel office in Namibia, "practically every male in the sending area" for the one copper mine on which he worked "has at one time or another engaged in contract labour, and all the migrants I interviewed anticipated that they would again take labour contracts in the future often after a stay of only one or two months at home." (Gordon op. cit. p. 217).

37.  Republic of South Africa, Bantu Investment Corporation, *Homelands—The Role of the Corporations*, Pretoria.

38.  John Kane-Berman op. cit. p. 5.

39.  *Towards Manpower Development for Namibia*, United Nations Institute for Namibia 1978, Table 2 p. 16.

John Kane-Berman has estimated that in 1971 contract workers constituted over 80% of the total black labour force (which he put at 50,000, a somewhat low figure). The International Labour Office and the United Nations Council for Namibia have also assumed that contract workers constitute about 80% of the labour force. (ILO, *Twelfth Special Report of the Director-General on the Application of the Declaration Concerning the Policy of Apartheid of the Republic of South Africa*, Geneva 1976 p. 38: *UN Council for Namibia Report* 1976 Vol. I p. 34).

A recent study in the United States, sponsored by the African–American Scholars Council under contract with the Agency for International Development has concluded that "no other country has such a high proportion of migrant workers in its labour force—even in South Africa only about 30% of the workers are migrants. The trend in Namibia is for the proportion of migrant workers to increase even further as more Africans are moved out of white areas and are forced to settle in the "homelands". (*Zimbabwe/Namibia—Anticipation of Economic and Humanitarian Needs—Transition Problems of Developing Nations in Southern Africa*, Final Report, March 1977 p. 191). Professor W. H. Thomas, however, has concluded that in the early 70's Ovambo contract workers constituted only 17% of the total Namibian labour force (presumably including both black and white) and that the importance of migrant labour may even have somewhat declined since, "as employers have gradually substituted Ovambo and Angolan migrants by locally resident blacks." (W. H. Thomas *Economic Development in Namibia*, op. cit., p. 287 n. 39). In the early 1970's the migratory labour force contained a substantial number of black workers from Angola, a flow which largely ceased with the advent of independence in 1975. In the absence of official statistics, estimates of the size of the labour force inevitably depend on a large degree of guesswork and also vary according to the definitions used.

40.  Republic of South Africa, Department of Labour *Manpower Survey 1975*, analysed in W. H. Thomas, *Economic Development in Namibia* op. cit. p. 196 ff.

In 1978, a total of 155 Namibians, mostly black and including Damaras, Hereros, Kavangos, Namas and Tswanas as well as Coloureds and Basters, were admitted to the South African Railways Training College at the Otjihase Mine near Windhoek, for intensive training to take over the future running of the railways in Namibia. A number of blacks were also admitted to an adjoining South African Railways Police College, for training as railway police constables. This project, significantly the first of its kind in Namibia, was prompted by the prospect of impending independence in Namibia (*WO* 19.8.78, *WA* 13.9.78).

41.  *Towards Manpower Development for Namibia — Background Notes*. United Nations Institute for Namibia 1978 p. 7.

42. There have been attempts by the authorities to alter this in recent years. Damara women for example began to be required to register following the 1971–72 strike (R. Voipio op. cit., January 1973).
43. *SALB* Vol. 4 Nos. 1 and 2, Jan–Feb. 1978.

44. W. H. Thomas, *Economic Development in Namibia* op. cit. p. 197 table 22.
45. UN *Decolonization Committee Report*, 29 September 1976, Ch. IV, Annex II.
46. ibid; W. H.. Thomas, *Economic Development in Namibia* op. cit. p. 198.

## III. THE EXPERIENCE OF THE BLACK WORKER

1. *RDM* 21.10.75.
2. Vagrancy Proclamation No. 25 of 1920, sections 1 and 3.
3. UN Department of Political Affairs, Trusteeship and Decolonization, *Decolonization* No. 9/Revised edition, December 1977, issue on Namibia.
4. Robert J. Gordon, *Mines, Masters and Migrants: Life in a Namibian Mine Compound*, Johannesburg, 1977 pp. 18–19.
5. The labour bureaux were introduced by the South African authorities as part of the concessions forced by a general strike of contract workers in 1971/72. They replaced the hated South West Africa Native Labour Association (SWANLA), and constituted a more decentralised recruitment system in the sense that authority for job allocation was devolved to the bantustans. While the labour bureaux and other reforms represented a softening of the old, highly rigid contract labour system they left its basic characteristics unchanged (see also Ch. VII).
6. Keith Gottschalk; *South African Labour Policy in Namibia* 1915–1975, in *SALB* Vol. 4 Nos. 1 and 2, Jan–Feb. 1978.
7. ibid.
8. R. Voipio, *The Labour Situation in South West Africa*, South African Institute of Race Relations, Johannesburg 1973 p. 9.
9. *SALB* Vol. 4 Nos. 1 and 2, Jan–Feb. 1978.
10. *Voipio* op. cit. p. 9.
11. *Die Suidwes Afrikaner* 27.7.73. In the aftermath of the contract workers strike in 1972 employers were reported to be recruiting their own men in Ovamboland and transporting them back to the south, but an order was soon issued by the authorities that workers had to travel by South African railways, bus or train. (*Voipio* op. cit. p. 3). More recently, however, the authorities appear to have been relaxing these restrictions.
12. Information given to authors by CDM in London. It seems that CDM may now be being joined by a number of other employers in this respect.
13. *SALB* Vol. 4 Nos. 1 and 2, Jan–Feb. 1978.
14. ibid.
15. ibid.
16. Gottschalk op. cit.
17. Rauha Voipio "*Kontrak-Soos die Owambo dit sien*", published January 1972 by the Evangelical Lutheran Church in Namibia; English translation of extracts of the report published as Appendix IV of John Kane-Berman *Contract Labour in South West Africa*. South African Institute of Race Relations, April 1972.
18. Kane-Berman op. cit. appendix II p. viii.

19. ibid. p. 17.
20. Gordon op. cit. p. 244–5.
21. *Constitutional Conference of South West Africa*, Cape Town 1976, pp. 19, 23–4, 37–8.
22. *Star* 28.8.76.
23. *WA* 2/14.9.77.
24. *GN* 22.10.77; *WA* 6.7.78.
25. *GN* 22.10.77.
26. *WA* 22.11.77. In reply to a question in the South African parliament in February 1978, the South African government confirmed that the following laws affecting labour had been repealed in Namibia:—
    ● Sections 5, 6, 7, 8, 9, 10, 11, 12 and 20(c) of the Native Administration Proclamation, 1922(Procl. 11 of 1922).
    ● Native Administration Amendment Proclamation,1927 (Procl. 11 of 1927).
    ● Prohibition of Credit to Natives Proclamation, 1927 (Procl. 18 of 1927).
    ● Prohibited Areas Proclamation, 1928 (Procl. 26 of 1928).
    ● Sections 10, 10 bis, 11, 12, 23, 25, 26, and 27 of the Natives (Urban Areas) Proclamation, 1951. (Procl. 56 of 1951). (*Debates* 14.2.78).
27. *FM* 11.11.77.
28. International Labour Office, *Labour and Discrimination in Namibia*, Geneva 1977, pp. 80–1; *see also fn.* 26.
29. *WA* 27.10.77.
30. *Constitutional Conference of South West Africa*, op. cit. pp. 19, 36–7.
31. *WA* 27.10.77.
32. *WA* 18.11.77. Similar allegations have been made by SWAPO and others inside Namibia over the last two years in connection with the issue of "supporters' cards" by the Turnhalle constitutional talks and by the political party, or rather federation of parties, subsequently formed out of the Turnhalle tribal delegations, the Democratic Turnhalle Alliance. Towards the end of 1978, furthermore, white employers were among those reported to be pressurising Namibians to register for South African-sponsored general elections (*see Appendix B*). (*FOCUS* 9 *p.* 15; 17 *p.* 9; 18 *p.* 16).
33. *WA* 1.12.77.
34. In October 1978, Windhoek's Director of Non-White Affairs, Mr Leon Venter, revealed that there were at that time about five applications a month to buy houses in the black township of Katutura. The new legal provisions enabling blacks to buy the land on which such houses stood were not expected to come into operation until the end of that year. (*WA* 26.10.78).

## IV. WAGES AND FRINGE BENEFITS

1. *SALB* Vol. 4 Nos. 1 and 2, Jan–Feb. 1978, p. 12–13.
   According to information supplied to the authors by the Chairman of Metal Box Overseas Ltd. in the UK, the basic wage of workers on the lowest paid grade at Metal Box South Africa Ltd. was R172.13 per month in July 1978. The same wage rates and conditions applied at the company's factory in Walvis Bay as at other plants in South Africa. (*Letter* dated 18.9.78).
2. *Towards Manpower Development for Namibia—Background Notes*, United Nations Institute for Namibia, 1978, p. 1.
3. *Report of the United Nations Council for Namibia*, Vol. 1, 1976, p. 33.
4. *ibid*. p. 34.
5. *SALB* op. cit. p. 98.
6. International Labour Office, *Labour and Discrimination in Namibia*, Geneva 1977, p. 61.
7. *WA* 21.7.78.
8. Rio Tinto-Zinc Corporation Ltd. *Fact Sheet No. 2 Some Aspects of Rössing Uranium Limited*, 18 May 1978.
9. John Kane-Berman *Contract Labour in South West Africa*, South African Institute of Race Relations, Johannesburg 1972, Appendix III p. xiii.
10. *SALB* op. cit. p. 14, interviews recorded in January 1977.
11. *SALB* op. cit. p. 20.
12. *SALB* op. cit. p. 21.
13. Peter Fraenkel, *The Namibians of South West Africa*, Minority Rights Group Report No. 19, New Edition, April 1978, p. 36.
14. *ibid.*; *SALB* op. cit. p. 97.
15. Fraenkel op. cit. p. 36.
16. United Nations Economic and Social Council, Commission on Human Rights *Situation of Human Rights in Southern Africa: Report of the Ad Hoc Working Group of Experts*, E/CN4/1222, 31 January 1977, p. 123; Murray et al op. cit., p. 141.
17. South African Department of Foreign Affairs, *South West Africa Survey* 1974.
18. *FM* 15.11.74.
19. Robert J. Gordon, *Mines, Masters and Migrants: Life in a Namibian Mine Compound*, Johannesburg 1977, p. 11.
20. *GN* 8.5.73.
21. *Decolonization Committee Report* op. cit., Annex II, p. 15.
22. *ibid*.
23. International Labour Office op. cit. p. 61.
24. Unpublished report July 1976.
25. *WA* 19.5.78.
26. Gordon op. cit. p. 195 note 7.
27. R. Voipio, *The Labour Situation in South West Africa*, South African Institute of Race Relations, Johannesburg 1973 p. 5.
28. *SALB* op. cit. p. 27.
29. International Labour Office op. cit. p. 69.
   In May 1977 the South African Minister of Coloured, Rehoboth and Nama Relations stated in reply to a parliamentary question that a total of 3,998 Coloured, Rehoboth Baster and Nama people in Namibia were receiving old age pensions, blind person's pensions or disability grants. The maximum amounts being paid were R38.50 per month in the case of Namas. (*Debates* 26.5.77).
30. *Constitutional Conference of South West Africa*, Cape Town, 1976, p. 29.
31. ibid. p. 27.
32. Evidence supplied to authors by BBC Television team.
33. *SALB* op. cit. p. 31.
34. United Nations Commission on Human Rights, *Progress Report of the Ad Hoc Working Group of Experts*, 31 January 1978 E/CN.4/1270, p. 118. The Turnhalle committee itself published information on current earnings in Namibia. In a document published in 1976, it divided workers into groups according to colour, sex and average earnings, and claimed that black unskilled workers were earning average wages of R77.80 a month throughout Namibia; semi-skilled R120.45 and skilled R172. Salaries of black workers employed in professional, clerical and administrative work were said to be between R240 and R462 a month. Although clearly on the high side, the figures given are not entirely outside the bounds of possibility for relatively well-paid jobs in mining or the tertiary sector, although even the minimum unskilled wage given in the document is about twice as high as the average paid in agriculture. The committee of the conference which produced these figures conceded that there could be truth in the argument that "the figures are not accurate because they reflect only averages", but argued that although the statistics were not "the be-all and end-all . . . they do give an indication of what the real situation is". The committee gave no definition of which workers fell into its skilled, semi-skilled and unskilled categories. It also claimed that the value of wages in kind—accommodation, food etc.—provided by the employer, amounted to some R50 a month. (*Constitutional Conference of South West Africa*, Cape Town 1976; *UN Commission on Human Rights* ibid).
35. *WA* 21.3.78. In an editorial comment on the day following the press conference, the *Windhoek Advertiser*, Namibia's main English-language daily, described Mr. Steenkamp's remarks on equal pay as a "senseless utterance". "We are also in a position to tell him", the editorial continued, "that he will have no say in wages in a new independent South West Africa

unless this Territory becomes a client
state of Pretoria and has a phony independence bestowed on it." (*ibid.* 22.3.78).
36. *WA* 21.3.78.
37. *WA* 3.4.78.
38. *WA* 14.6.78, 15.6.78.
39. *WA* 19.6.78.
40. International Labour Office op. cit. p. 52.

41. *WA* 15.6.78.
42. *WO* 9.9.78.
43. *WO* 28.10.78.
44. *BBC* 28. 10.78. Later reports stated that
equal pay for equal work would be introduced in the public sector at the end of
November 1978 (*RDM* 20.11.78).

## V. PARTICULAR INDUSTRIES

1. South African Department of Foreign
Affairs, *South West Africa Survey* 1974.
2. *UN Decolonization Committee Report*, 24
October 1975, Part III, Annex p. 31.
3. Robert J. Gordon, *Mines, Masters and
Migrants: Life in a Namibian Mine Compound*, Johannesburg 1977, p. 195 n.6.
4. Interview with authors in London.
5. Gordon op. cit. p. 89.
6. Peter Fraenkel, *The Namibians of South
West Africa*, Minority Rights Group
Report No. 19, New Edition, April 1978,
p. 37.
7. US Committee on Foreign Affairs, *US
Business Involvement in Southern Africa*,
part 2, Washington 1972, p. 345.
8. *US Business Involvement in Southern
Africa* op. cit. pp. 87–88.
9. *Breaking Contract—The Story of Vinnia
Ndadi*, ed. Dennis Mener, LSM Press
1974, pp. 97–8.
10. Fraenkel op. cit. p. 37.
11. *Anglo American Corporation Base Metals
Division. Investigation into Tsumeb Corporation Limited, May 1975. Memorandum
for Mr. G. Langton by J. Ainsworth, 6 June
1975, Johannesburg, JA/KM. Document
P.—from Renfrew Christie, Research
Report Tsumeb Corporation Limited,
Namibia. Excerpts from Documents prepared by officials of the Anglo-American
Corporation of South Africa Limited in
1975* (henceforth referred to as Christie,
*Research Report*).
12. Christie, *Research Report*, Documents
Q & R.
13. *Namibia*, December 1977, Israeli TV and
VARA TV Netherlands.
14. Fraenkel op. cit. p. 37, quoting BBC TV
"Panorama" programme of 28 March
1977. In June 1976, the De Beers group
announced wage increases for black
workers employed on both its South
African and Namibian mines. Minimum
basic wages would range from R92.50 to
R105.10 per month with effect from 1
June 1976. Rates in the top operating
category were increased to R406 per
month. The group estimated that the
average basic wage including increments
for service would now stand at R134.82
per month. (*FT* 10.6.76).
15. *GN* 8.5.73.
16. Information from BBC Television team.
17. Information from BBC TV team.
18. According to the BBC "Panorama" team
which visited CDM in early 1977, 24
houses were being built for black workers'

families by the company, of which six
were ready but stood empty. The team
were told that the plan to offer these
houses to workers and their families from
the "homelands" had received a set-back
due to resistance from the Ovambo tribal
authorities. The latter are thought to fear
that permanent outward migration would
mean a loss of political authority and also
of income. This suggestion is supported
by a statement in the 1976 *Annual Report*
of the Tsumeb Corporation, that, in rela-
tion to proposals to provide family housing, "the Corporation still awaits a response to approaches made to the Chief
Minister of Ovamboland, to allow Ovambo
families to take up residence at Tsumeb."
(*p.* 1). In December 1978 the *Windhoek
Advertiser* reported however that the
Oranjemund Primary School would be
opened to black pupils for the first time
in 1979. 50 children of black families
accommodated at the mine would attend
classes along with whites in a pioneering
attempt at racial integration. Most of
them were the children of Ovambos employed at CDM, who previously had been
separated from their families by the
migrant labour system. (*WA* 4.12.78).
    The 1976 *Annual Report* of the New-
mont Mining Corporation states that at
Tsumeb, "Up to 100 houses for Ovambo
employees and their families have been
authorised by the South West African
Government. . . . The Company's objective in arranging for family residence is to
create a more stable and skilled work force.
Under the present system, African employees stay at the mine on single status
for relatively short periods. This results
in high turnover and makes training
difficult." (*p.* 4). The type of housing
being provided at Tsumeb certainly
sounds preferable to the dormitory accommodation hitherto general: "Each
house has two or three bedrooms, living-
dining room, kitchen and modern bathroom." (p. 4). By the end of 1976, the
first 117 houses were according to the
company nearing completion.
19. Interviews recorded by Pastor Gerson
Max, Minister responsible for the United
Evangelical Church's mission to contract
workers in Namibia, among CDM
workers, 19 October, 1976.
20. ibid.
21. Interview with authors in London.
22. *US Business Involvement in Southern*

*Africa*, op. cit. p. 345.
23. B. Rogers, *Notes on Labour Conditions at the Rössing Mine, SALB* Vol. 4 Nos. 1 and 2, Jan–Feb. 1978, p. 140. Other companies operating in Namibia have publicly acknowledged the value of having a stable workforce. CDM officials in London, for example, told the authors that they would have no objections to a relaxation in the system of labour influx control and the emergence of a permanent non-migratory labour force. In practice this seems a most unlikely prospect while the South African authorities remain committed to a bantustan blueprint for Namibia's development. No amount of family housing provided by employers, however, philanthropic, is in itself going to produce 'settled communities' while the contract system prevails (see also note 18 above).
24. B. Rogers, op. cit.
In September 1978, the office of the SWA Administrator General announced that all "black areas" of Namibia—presumably a reference to the "homelands"—had been opened up for prospecting. An official said that such prospectors would have to make "exclusive use" of local labour unless they could satisfy the Administrator General that suitable labour was not available. A training programme for workers would also have to be introduced, he added. (*BBC* 6.9.78). While this announcement can perhaps be interpreted to indicate official concern at the bad image presented by Namibia's contract labour system, it seems unlikely to affect more than a minority of black workers in practice—since the "homelands" have been deliberately sited in areas devoid of obvious natural resources. Prospectors at this stage are presumably hoping to uncover minerals previously overlooked by the architects of the Odendaal Plan.
25. ibid.
26. RTZ *Fact Sheet No. 2* 1977; RTZ brochure *Rössing* 78, p. 27; RTZ Fact Sheet No. 2, 1978 "*Some Aspects of Rössing Uranium Ltd.*" (London 18 May 1978).
27. Information from BBC TV team. Some Ovambos who smuggled their families in were reportedly arrested and sent back north. (*B. Rogers op. cit.*). In May 1978 RTZ itself reported that "currently 424 houses (at Arandis) are occupied by married employees and their families. 933 single-status employees and contractors' employees engaged on Arandis contracts occupy a further 134 houses. In addition 20 other houses are occupied by families who are not associated with the company". By this time only 21 houses were standing vacant, according to the company. (*Fact Sheet No. 2*, May 1978). RTZ has admitted that "the task of training and acclimatising the local people to an industrial lifestyle has proved more difficult

than originally foreseen. Consequently black workers with some industrial experience from the north are being employed and living on a single status." (*Fact Sheet No. 2*, May 1977).
28. B. Rogers op. cit.
29. Notes taken by authors.
30. RTZ *Fact Sheet No. 2*, May 1978.
31. RTZ *Fact Sheet No. 2*, 1977 and Fact Sheet No. 2, 1976, quoted in B. Rogers, op. cit.
32. B. Rogers op. cit.
33. RTZ *Fact Sheet No. 2*, May 1978.
34. Colin Winter: "*Namibia—the story of a Bishop in Exile*" Lutterworth Press 1977, p. 153.
35. *RDM* 25.5.76; *WA* 24.5.76.
36. *SALB* op. cit. p. 13.
37. South African Department of Foreign Affairs, *South West Africa Survey* 1974.
38. *WA* 14.6.76.
39. *Star* 12.6.76.
40. Fraenkel. op. cit. p. 38.
41. *SALB* op. cit. p. 12.
42. *WA* 19.1.77.
43. Information compiled by Pastor Gerson Max; see also Ch. IV p. 471.
44. *SALB* op. cit. p. 45.
45. R. Voipio, *The Labour Situation in South West Africa*, South African Institute of Race Relations, Johannesburg 1973, p. 6.
46. *SALB* op. cit. p. 47.
47. Voipio op. cit. p. 8.
48. Information compiled by Pastor Gerson Max; see also Ch. IV p. 471.
49. John Kane-Berman, *Contract Labour in South West Africa*, South African Institute of Race Relations, Johannesburg 1972 p.15.
50. Kane Berman-op. cit. p. 19.
51. Judge William Booth, report to the International Commission of Jurists, March 1972; quoted in Colin Winter op. cit. p. 165–6.
52. Quoted in J. H. P. Serfontein, *Namibia ?* Randburg, South Africa, 1976, p. 219.
53. Kane-Berman op. cit. appendix III, p. xii.
54. Kane-Berman op. cit. p. 15–17, and appendix III, p. xii.
55. *SALB* op. cit. p. 17 ff.
56. Interview recorded by authors.
57. Students Representative Council, Bulletin of the Wages Commission, University of Cape Town, South Africa, 1972, p. 8–9.
58. Interview recorded by authors.
In November 1978, employers were required to pay R1.35 per day for a room in the new Katutura hostel and two meals, for each worker registered there. A new kitchen, equipped to cater for a maximum of 10,000 people and presided over by a Swiss-trained hotelier, had just been opened and, according to the hostel manager, was prepared to provide *a la carte* menus for residents for an extra fee. According to the *Windhoek Advertiser*, this "extremely modern food factory" looked "like a scene from *Willy Wonka*

116

and the Chocolate Factory . . . except that it is neat enough to seem deserted and very clean. . . . The quality of the food at present may or may not be questionable, but there can certainly be no complaints about quantity. Each resident receives a daily allowance of 3,674.5 kilojoules. This includes meat 310g, vegetables mielie-meal, rice, soup, vegetables, fresh fruit and tea." (*WA* 17.11.78).

Following its official closure, windows in the old hostel in Katutura were bricked up with the intention of using the buildings for storage purposes. Water installations and power cables were also removed. By September 1978, however, a total of 2,500 people were estimated to be living in the hostel as illegal squatters. Many of them were the victims of the mounting unemployment that had been affecting Windhoek since the beginning of the year. Others, including many SWAPO supporters, had been moved into the old hostel by the authorities in March during outbreaks of violence in the Katutura township (*see Chapter VIII*). The squatters also included many women and children.

At the beginning of September, the Windhoek Municipality declared that the old hostel constituted a health hazard and gave the squatters a fortnight's notice to leave the premises. They were duly evicted and the hostel buildings razed to the ground at a cost of R10,600—despite an offer from the squatters' representatives to repair and clean up the place and to pay rent for their accommodation once it had been made fit for human habitation. No alternative arrangements were provided by the authorities for the squatters, many of whom were subsequently discovered to be sleeping rough or living in homemade shanties on farms on the outskirts of Windhoek. (*WA* 8/19/27.10.78, *WO* 28.10.78).

59. South African Department of Foreign Affairs, *South West Africa Survey 1974*, p. 58.
60. Bettina Gebhardt, *The Socio-Economic Status of Farm Labourers in SWA/Namibia*, SALDRU Farm Labour Conference, University of Cape Town, September 1976; reprinted in *SALB* op. cit.
61. Gebhardt op. cit.
62. Gebhardt op. cit. A spokesman for the South West Africa Agricultural Union told a committee of the Turnhalle constitutional conference in 1976 that the number of workers from Ovambo, Kavango and Angola employed in agriculture had declined from 16,000 to 7,000. "Wages alone did not cause this tendency", the spokesman said, "but all the same play a very important part". (*Constitutional Conference of South West Africa*, Cape Town 1976).
63. *WA* 25.3.76.
64. *ibid.*; also *RDM* 26.3.76.
65. *WA* 24.2.77.
66. Interview with Namibian farm worker, 1977. *SALB* op. cit. pp. 14–15.
67. ibid. pp. 16–17.
68. Interviews recorded by the authors in London, 1977 (names fictitious).
69. Gebhardt op. cit.
70. Voipio op. cit. p. 6.
71. Gebhardt op. cit.
72. *South West Africa Constitutional Conference*, op. cit. pp. 72–3.
73. Gebhardt op. cit.
74. *Breaking Contract—The Story of Vinnia Ndadi* op. cit. p. 23.
75. *Tel* 4.2.72.

## VI.  THE RIGHT TO ORGANISE

1. *SALB* Vol. 4 Nos. 1 and 2, Jan–Feb. 1978, p.3.
2. *WA* 19.1.77.
3. *SALB* op. cit. p. 90.
4. International Labour Office, *Labour and Discrimination in Namibia*, Geneva 1977, p. 72. In South Africa itself, the *Bantu Labour (Settlement of Disputes) Act* of 1953 placed a total and explicit prohibition on strikes, go-slows, and similar action by African workers, under extremely severe penalties. This act, together with the *Industrial Conciliation Act* of 1956, was never extended to Namibia, however. In 1977, African workers in South Africa were granted the formal right to strike, but subject to so many restrictions as to be virtually meaningless.
5. *WA* 21.3.78.
6. Information supplied by CDM's office in London.
7. Students' Representative Council, Bulletin of the Wages Commission, University of Cape Town, South Africa, 1972, p. 4.
8. Ruaha Voipio; *The Labour Situation in South West Africa*, South African Institute of Race Relations, Johannesburg 1973, p.9.
9. John Kane-Berman, *Contract Labour in South West Africa*, South African Institute of Race Relations, Johannesburg 1972, p. 9.
10. Kane-Berman op. cit. p. 9.
11. ibid. p. 10.
12. *Constitutional Conference of South West Africa*, Cape Town 1976, p. 69.
13. *SALB* op. cit. p. 34.
14. RTZ Corporation *Fact Sheet No. 2 Some Aspects of Rössing Uranium Limited*, London 18.5.78.
15. *SALB* op. cit. p. 33.
16. ibid. p. 37–8, a black worker interviewed in 1977.
17. Proclamation No. AG 45 *Wage and Industrial Conciliation Amendment Proclamation*, 1978.

18. *WA* 12.7.78.
19. Proclamation No. AG 45 op. cit. Section 1: *Amendment of section 25 of Ordinance*

35 *of* 1952.
20. *FOCUS* 18 p. 14.
21. *FM* 1.9.78.

## VII. RESISTANCE—THE 1971/72 STRIKE

1. Quoted in R. J. Gordon; *A Note on the History of Labour Action in Namibia*, *SALB* Vol. 1 No. 10, April 1975.
2. ibid.
3. ibid.
4. ibid.
5. R. Voipio, *The Labour Situation in South West Africa*, South African Institute of Race Relations, Johannesburg 1973, p. 13.
6. *Sechaba*, official organ of the African National Congress of South Africa, Vol. 6, no. 4. April 1972, p. 22.
7. John Kane-Berman, *Contract Labour in South West Africa*, South African Institute of Race Relations, Johannesburg 1972, Appendix III.
8. R. J. B. Moorsom, *Worker Consciousness and the 1971–72 Contract Workers' Strike*, *SALB* Vol. 4 Nos. 1 and 2, Jan–Feb. 1978.
9. ibid.
10. *The Price of Liberation*, excerpts from the life history of Hinananje Shafodino Nehova, recorded by Ole Gjerstad; in *Namibia: SWAPO fights for freedom*, LSM Information Centre, California, 1978, p. 72.
11. Colin Winter: *Namibia—The Story of a Bishop in Exile*, Lutterworth Press 1977, p. 119.
12. R. J. B. Moorsom, op. cit., quoting Hinananje Nehova. As a student in Namibia, Nehova, along with others, had been expelled from high school in Ovamboland in August 1971 for demonstrating against the regime.
13. Randolph Vigne, *A Dwelling Place of our Own, The Story of the Namibian Nation*, IDAF 1973, p. 43. According to R. J. B. Moorsom, op. cit., nearly 19,000 workers had been involved in strike action by mid-January 1972, while at least 21,000 had been involved in some form of protest at a total of 23 centres, 11 of them mines.
14. R. J. B. Moorsom, op. cit.
15. R. J. B. Moorsom op. cit. p. 134.
16. *T* 12.12.71.
17. *BBC*, reporting a broadcast from Johannesburg 17.1.72. A fortnight earlier, however, Johannesburg radio had claimed that 500 workers were required on the railways (*BBC*, reporting Johannesburg broadcast 1.1.72).
18. *BBC*, reporting Johannesburg broadcast, 1.1.72. Hinananje Nehova, a contract worker and former student militant, stated that after the strike an attempt to use strike breakers from South Africa was a "total failure". (R. J. B. Moorsom, op. cit.
19. *BBC* reporting Johannesburg broadcast 22.12.71.

20. *BBC*, reportng Johannesburg broadcast 20.12.71.
21. IDAF *Information Service* Jan–June 1972, p. 523.
22. Colin Winter, *Namibia: The Story of a Bishop in Exile*, Lutterworth Press 1977, p. 119–120.
23. Extract from a notice issued by the strikers' leaders on 15 December. The notice, together with letters from workers at Walvis Bay to others in Windhoek, the diary of one of the activists in the Katutura compound, and other material relating to the strike and describing the events from the workers' point of view, were produced as exhibits in the subsequent trial of 12 alleged strike leaders. Detailed extracts from these documents are reproduced in *SALB* Vol. 4 nos. 1 and 2, Jan–Feb. 1978, pp. 181 ff.
24. IDAF *Information Service* Jan–June 1972, p. 524. Inquest documents on eight Africans killed in January became available for the first time on 24 June 1972. The station commander at Oshikango on the Angolan border said in an affidavit that efforts by the authorities to recruit Chimbundu workers from Angola to replace Ovambo strikers had been fiercely resisted by the Ovambos. Police had baton charged the Ovambos, who had armed themselves with pangas, knives and other weapons.
25. John Kane-Berman, op. cit.
26. *Obs.* 4.11.73.
27. IDAF *Information Service* Jan–June 1972, p. 524; *Debates* 6.2.73/10.4.73, quoted in R.J.B. Moorsom, op. cit.
28. *WA* 26.6.72.
29. Extracts from *Statement on the Epinga shootings*, issued 7 February 1972 by Colin O'Brien Winter, Bishop of Damaraland, and reproduced in full in Colin Winter, op. cit., p. 132.
30. IDAF *Information Service* Jan–June 1972, p. 524.
31. Colin Winter op. cit. p. 139.
32. *T* 3.2.72.
33. ibid.
34. R. J. B. Moorsom, op. cit.
35. The bantustan tribal officials and headmen, in particular, were seen as willing collaborators with the apartheid regime. Headman Filippus Kaluvi, for example, was before the strike "appointed as liaison official between the Ovambo government and the contract-workers. Although the Ovambos, as far as I know, originally had nothing against him personally, it became impossible for him to carry out his task. He was the personification of the hated system. It is reported from Windhoek

that he refused, because of fear, to enter the Ovambo compound, or even to address a meeting in church. Those who told me of this were of the opinion that headman Kaluvi had reason to be afraid. He then got the answer from a few individuals that the men were satisfied, and he reported this view." (Voipio, op. cit. p. 12).

36. IDAF *Information Service*, July–December 1971, p. 491.
37. BBC reporting Johannesburg broadcast, 20.1.72.
38. ibid.
39. BBC reporting Johannesburg broadcast, 21.1.72.
40. IDAF *Information Service* Jan–June 1972, p. 524; Colin Winter op. cit. p. 124–5. The *Masters and Servants Proclamation* and other indenture legislation was repealed by Proclamation 105 (1975).
41. John Kane-Berman, op. cit. pp. 16–17.
42. *Tel* 25.1.72. Whatever the reasons, Nangatuuala's announcement was not taken at its face value. "When, near the end of January, the chairman of the strike committee ill-advisedly welcomed the new form of migratory labour and urged strikers to go back, using the local radio station to reach a wider audience than he had ever had, the people largely ignored

him, not only because his judgement was so clearly wrong as to the merits of the proposed tribal recruiting scheme, but also because in their eyes he had no mandate to accept it." (*Sechaba*, official organ of the African National Congress of South Africa, Vol. 6 No. 4, April 1972, pp. 23–4). Mr. Nangatuuala later said that the government had broken the promises it made at Grootfontein (*WA* 7.7.72). He was later arrested and imprisoned for his activities in organising an opposition party in Ovamboland and in October 1973, was hospitalised after receiving 20 lashes in a public flogging. In 1976 he disappeared—he was said by the South African authorities to have been abducted by SWAPO and taken to Angola.

43. Kane-Berman op. cit. p. 13; *T* 1.3.72.
44. *T* 18.3.72.
45. *T* 2.3.72.
46. *Tel* 6.4.72.
47. Keith Gottschalk, *South African Labour Policy in Namibia* 1915–1975, in *SALB* op. cit. p. 93.
48. Voipio op. cit. p. 6–7.
49. Kane-Berman op. cit. p. 8.
50. Keith Gottschalk, op. cit.
51. *Christian Science Monitor* 1.3.72, quoted in Vigne op. cit. p. 44.

## VIII. THE APARTHEID RESPONSE—DIVIDE AND RULE

1. IDAF *Information Service* Jan–June 1972 p. 524.
2. Ruaha Voipio, *The Labour Situation in South West Africa*, South African Institute of Race Relations, Johannesburg, January 1973.
3. For a detailed account of the setting-up of the Turnhalle constitutional talks, and South Africa's continuing attempts to entrench bantustans in Namibia, see *All Options and None—The Constitutional Talks in Namibia*, IDAF Fact Paper No. 3, August 1976. More recent developments have been covered in IDAF's bi-monthly news bulletin *FOCUS on Political Repression in Southern Africa*, in particular the setting up of so-called "homeland armies" in Ovamboland and Kavangoland and the recruiting of Namibians from other "population groups" for military service on tribal lines.
4. GN 20.11.76.
5. See Ch. V.
6. GN 19.11.76.
7. *SALB* Vol. 4 Nos. 1 and 2, Jan–Feb. 1978, p. 39, GN 23.11.76.
8. B. Rogers. *Notes on Labour Conditions at the Rössing Mine, SALB* op. cit. p. 141.
9. ibid. p. 142.
10. GN 19/20.11.76.
11. GN 23.11.76.
12. See Ch. V.
13. *SALB* op. cit. p. 10.
14. ibid. p. 40–41.
15. *WA* 8.7.75.
16. *WA* 23.7.75.
17. *FOCUS* No. 8, January 1977, p. 14.
18. *FOCUS* No. 9, March 1977, p. 16 and No. 10, May 1977, p. 17.
19. *SALB* op. cit. p. 49 ff.
20. ibid. p. 50.
21. *FOCUS* No. 8, January 1977, p. 14.
22. *FOCUS* No. 9, March 1977, p. 17. In October 1976 Captain Witbooi had led the Witbooi section of the Namas, together with three other groups representing almost 10,000 Namas *in toto*, to join SWAPO. He was later appointed SWAPO's Secretary for Education and Culture inside Namibia. In May 1978 he was arrested together with dozens of other SWAPO members and officials, in a countrywide purge by the police, and held in detention without charge for nearly two months.
23. *SALB* op. cit. pp. 57–8.
24. *Sunday News*, Tanzania 3.7.77.
25. *FOCUS* No. 16, May 1978, p. 6.
26. *WA* 1.3.78.
27. *FOCUS* No. 16, May 1978, p. 7.
28. *WA* 13.1.78.
29. *WA* 8.3.78.
30. *FOCUS* No. 16, May 1978, p. 7.
31. *RDM* 2.2.78.
32. Swakopmund Municipality, *Special Circular—Matters concerning Labour*, dated 2 February 1976, in Afrikaans, English and German.
33. *WA* 1.3.78.

34. *MS* 2.3.78; also Peter Katjavivi, SWAPO Publicity Secretary, in interview with authors.
35. *WA* 1.3.78.
36. *WA* 2.3.78.
37. ibid.
38. *WA* 7.3.78. In SWAPO's view, responsibility for the violence and loss of life lay squarely with the South African government, which had "engineered an excuse for their collaborators from the Turnhalle to go on the rampage and indiscriminately beat up individual members and supporters of SWAPO. . . . At no time was any attempt made by the South African police to disarm these thugs or to intervene. Instead they offered their support and backing and have thus enabled the violence to continue and spread." (*Statement issued in London on* 7 March 1978 by Peter Katjavivi, SWAPO Secretary for Information and Publicity).
39. *FOCUS* No. 16, May 1978, p. 6.
40. *FOCUS* ibid. p. 7.
41. *WA* 7.3.78.
42. *WA* 8.3.78. White employers had little sympathy with the strike. The Managing Director of South West Breweries, for example, confirmed that his firm would be replacing any workers who had stayed away, from the ranks of the unemployed. The owner of a local butchery urged the authorities to "deprive [the strikers] of food and water, and we will soon see who wants to work and who does not want to work". (*WA* ibid.).
43. *WA* 8.3.78. In a statement issued during March 1978 "on behalf of the Namibian workers" by SWAPO's secretary for Labour, Mr. Jason Angula, it was pointed out that workers who had travelled to Windhoek and the south could "only do our work properly if our safety is ensured. If our services are no longer needed in this country this should have been put directly to us. By shooting and beating us with rifle butts you are indirectly telling us that we are living in a fool's paradise by believing that we can still live and work in peace under these circumstances . . . we as workers and at the same time members of SWAPO who have been experiencing all these brutal activities of Kapuuo's clique, the babies of the oppressors, have therefore decided to stay away from work in order to avoid more bloodshed . . . should any one of us be dismissed [for staying away from work], then the whole compound will go on strike again, because he did not stay away from work because of his own problem but because of a national one. In future, peace on the labour scene will totally depend on the impartiality of the South African police.

"We can only help building this country if our services are fully appreciated and our safety well protected".
44. *WA* 16.3.78.
45. *FOCUS* No. 16, May 1978, p. 6.
46. *WA* 21.3.78.
47. *FOCUS* No. 17, July 1978, p. 10–11. While South African spokesmen claimed that the arrests had been necessitated by the assassination of Chief Kapuuo and the general threat to law and order posed by SWAPO's activities, little or no concrete evidence was ever produced by the authorities as to the Chief's killers. In September 1978 an official judicial inquiry into the murder found that Chief Kapuuo had been shot dead by "persons unknown". (*WA* 26.9.78).

## IX. UNITY IS STRENGTH

1. *SALB* Vol. 4 Nos. 1 and 2, Jan–Feb. 1978, pp. 44–5.
2. *Debates,* 18 April 1975, col. 4381.
3. *Breaking Contract—The Story of Vinnia Ndadi,* recorded and edited by Dennis Mercer, Life Histories from the Revolution No. 1, LSM Press, Canada 1974, p. 64.
4. The OPO was originally known as the Ovamboland People's Congress but changed its name to OPO in 1958.
5. Colin Winter, *Namibia—the Story of a Bishop in Exile,* Lutterworth Press 1977, p. 185 ff.
6. R. J. B. Moorsom, *Worker Consciousness and the* 1971–72 *Contract Workers' Strike,* in *SALB* op. cit. p. 127.
7. *SWAPO Information on SWAPO: An Historical Profile,* issued by SWAPO Department of Information and Publicity, July 1978.
8. *Breaking Contract,* op. cit. pp. 64–5.
9. R. J. B. Moorsom, *SALB* op. cit. p. 128.
10. *Breaking Contract* op. cit. pp. 85–6.
11. ibid. p. 92.
12. ibid. p. 92–3.
13. Interview recorded by authors (full name withheld).
14. Interview recorded by authors (full name withheld).
15. Robert J. Gordon, *Mines, Masters and Migrants—Life in a Namibian Mine Compound,* Johannesburg 1977, p. 19–20.
16. ibid.
17. *Information on the People's Resistance* 1976–77, SWAPO Department of Information and Publicity, July 1978, p. 12.
18. ibid.
19. Interviews with authors.
20. *WO* 26.8.78.
21. R. J. B. Moorsom, *SALB* op cit. p. 129. SWAPO's own political programme recognises that the "close historic identification of our movement with the interests of the toiling masses of the Namibian people is one of the main factors which explain the resilience of our movement when compared to other anti-

colonial groups which had emerged in Namibia and have either collapsed or remained paper organisations." (*Political Program of the South West Africa People's Organisation (SWAPO) of Namibia*, adopted by the meeting of the Central Committee, July 28–August 1, 1976, Lusaka, Zambia).

22. R. J. B. Moorsom, *SALB*, op. cit. p. 129.
23. *SALB* op. cit. p. 190.
24. *Sunday News*, Tanzania, 3.7.77.
25. Report prepared by Eric Sjöquist, editor of *Expressen*, for the Lutheran World Federation. LWF Information 41/77 16 November 1977. Pastor Gerson Max, referred to in the extract, is the Minister responsible for the United Evangelical Church's mission to contract workers.
26. Interview with authors, March 1978.
27. *BBC* 24 November 1978, *WA* 24 November 1978.
28. *Report on the Registration and Election Campaign in Namibia*, 1978, Christian Centre in Namibia, 28 November 1978.
29. *FM* 8 December 1978.

# Appendix A

## Draft Constitution of the Namibian Workers' Union (NAWU)

### NAME
The name of the Union shall be NAMIBIAN WORKERS' UNION, hereinafter referred to as NAWU.

### HEADQUARTERS
The Headquarters of NAWU shall be situated in Windhoek, or at any other such place as the Executive Committee may decide from time to time.

### AIMS AND OBJECTS
(a) Generally to organise and protect from exploitation and look after the interests of all workers in various job categories in Namibia.

(b) To create unity and solidarity among all workers in Namibia.

(c) To pave the way and prepare for a participation by the workers of Namibia in the Government of an independent Namibia.

(d) To make the workers of Namibia conscious of the present system of labour and do everything in their power to strive for better and equal working and living conditions.

(e) Insofar as this is compatible with a Workers' Union to take part and contribute to a complete change in the present social, economic and political order, and do everything in their power to achieve this.

(f) To oppose all tribalism and ethnic grouping as well as all types of discrimination among Namibian workers, and fight for the abolishment of all barriers of estrangement presently existing.

(g) To make a study in depth of all problems of the workers and find ways of solving them.

(h) To fight for the dignity of all workers.

(i) To do everything in its power to achieve economic equality in any future Government of Namibia.

(j) To co-operate with other Workers' Unions having basically the same aims and objects.

(k) To fight for just wages, good working conditions and to protect the interests of all workers.

(l) To regulate relations, negotiate and settle disputes between workers and employers.

(m) To provide advice and or obtain legal assistance where necessary for workers or matters affecting their employment.

## MEMBERSHIP

(a) Membership shall be open to all workers of Namibia irrespective of trade, craft or job, race, religion or sex.

(b) Membership shall be by individual affiliation only.

(c) A worker shall be deemed a member of the union on payment of a joining fee, which shall be one Rand until changed by the Executive Committee.

(d) The Executive Committee shall have the right to accept or reject membership.

(e) Whenever practicable membership cards shall be issued.

## RESIGNATION

A member who intends to resign his membership must submit his resignation in writing to the Union's Executive Committee. Furthermore, he must give reasons as to why he has decided to resign. Unreasonable resignations will not be accepted.

## EXECUTIVE COMMITTEE

(a) Chairman.

(b) Deputy-Chairman.

(c) Secretary-General.

(d) Vice Secretary—General.

(e) Treasurer.

(f) Vice-Treasurer.

(g) Three additional committee members.

## DUTIES

(*The duties of the Executive Committee, Chairman, Deputy Chairman, Secretary. General, Vice Secretary-General, Treasurer and Vice-Treasurer are specified.*)

## THE CONGRESS

There shall be an annual congress, to be convened by the Executive Committee- All branches of the Union shall send delegations to the Congress which shall be the Supreme Authority of the Union.

## THE BRANCH EXECUTIVE COMMITTEE
(a) Branch Chairman.
(b) Secretary.
(c) Treasurer.
(d) Six additional members.

## DUTIES
### Branch Chairman
(a) He shall represent the Union at that particular Branch.
(b) He shall lead the delegation of that Branch to the Congress.

### Branch Secretary
(a) He shall be responsible for all correspondence of the Union for his branch.
(b) He shall keep lists of members of his Branch and shall send copies to the Secretary-General.
(c) He shall be the organiser of his Branch.

### Branch Treasurer
(a) He shall keep all the money of his Branch.
(b) He shall raise funds for his Branch.

### The Additional Members
They shall assist the Chairman, Secretary and Treasurer in the execution of their duties.

## CELLS
The Branch shall be divided into cells. Members of the Union who are working together shall form a cell at that factory, farm, mine, etc.
(Taken from *South African Labour Bulletin*, Vol. 4, Nos. 1 and 2 January-February 1978, p. 190 ff.).

# Appendix B

## The December 1978 Elections

From 4-8 December 1978, the South African government organised general elections in Namibia in defiance of the United Nations and of international opinion. The purpose was to install the Democratic Turnhalle Alliance (DTA) as a proxy government in the territory, as a counterbalance to the national liberation movement SWAPO, and to win further concessions for South Africa in the bargaining with the West over Namibia's future. Massive resources were expended by the South African authorities in organising an American presidential-style election campaign to promote the DTA, which in due course secured 41 out of 50 seats in a Constituent Assembly set up in the territory at the end of December.

The elections however were boycotted not only by SWAPO, but by other political parties in Namibia opposed to apartheid and to South African government policies. (Besides the DTA, four parties put up candidates for the Constituent Assembly. Two were extreme right wing white groups, the other two small splinter groups). Since the South African government's claim to be in Namibia at all was withdrawn in 1966 by the United Nations General Assembly, it had no right in international law to organise the elections in the first place. The methods used to force the black majority to the polls, furthermore, must be seen in the light of the fact that Namibia is a country occupied by up to 60,000 foreign troops and run as a police state. Both polling, and the registration of voters which preceded it, took place under martial law conditions. The arrest, on the eve of the elections, of six key members of SWAPO's national executive in Namibia together with 80 members of its Youth League, put the liberation movement's Windhoek office out of action at a crucial time. Extensive evidence was collected by Namibian church organizations, as well as SWAPO itself, of large scale irregularities, threats and intimidation by the South African authorities and by the political parties taking part in the elections, notably the DTA. All these factors explain why the South African government was later able to announce a poll of over 80% of registered voters and to claim that black Namibians had come forward with eagerness to take part in the elections. As far as black workers were concerned, it is clear that the threat of the sack, the fear of being unable to find work, or the loss of wages and benefits, were crucial to the high turnout.

### Registration of voters

On 20 June 1978, the SWA Administrator General, Justice Steyn, announced that registration of voters for general elections in Namibia would take place from

26 June to 22 September. (In the event, the registration period was extended well into October—one of the many factors which helped to ensure that according to South African government claims, more than 92% of the eligible population were finally registered to vote). Potential voters of all racial groups had to be at least 18 years of age and to have been born in Namibia or have lived there for at least four years.

According to Justice Steyn, the decision to begin registration was "an essentially neutral step of an administrative nature" and a "necessary preparation" for the free general elections envisaged in Namibia under the terms of the settlement proposals put forward by the five Western members of the UN Security Council. This assertion was denied by the Western power themselves[1]. The move was seen by observers as a direct snub to the stipulation of UN member states that any elections in Namibia must be under United Nations supervision and control. It soon became clear that the registration process would be anything but "neutral". Shortly before the Administrator General's announcement, the Chief of the South African Defence Force in Namibia, Major-General Jannie Geldenhuys, warned that registration would "place a heavy burden on the Defence Force to ensure security in the Operational Area to make registration possible"[2].

On 13 June, new controls over freedom of movement were imposed on northern Namibia by Justice Steyn, prohibiting vehicular travel at night except with the written consent of the South African authorities. In effect, the measures amounted to a return to the state of emergency imposed on the north during the 1971/72 contract workers' strike and only partially relaxed in November 1977.[3] The second half of 1978 saw a considerable build-up of South African Defence Force personnel and police in northern Namibia, with continued violations of Angola's southern border by South African troops.[4]

White employers, for their part, co-operated closely with the South African authorities during the registration process. In October, for example, the *Windhoek Observer* reported that "certain firms are firing workers for not having registered. There seems to be the idea that a man is a traitor unless he has registered and supports either the DTA or Aktur".[5] (Aktur, an extreme right wing, all-white party, won 6 out of the 50 seats in the December elections.) Later, the paper's political columnist commented that she had received calls from people all over Namibia "who believe they have to vote, and if not they could be penalised by means of a heavy fine. Many employers have allegedly been asking for registration cards before they will employ a certain person".[6]

In a statement issued by its Secretary of Publicity and Information, SWAPO also alleged that: "The so-called electoral process including the voters' registration has involved wide-scale intimidation and harassment of the Namibian people. Thousands continue to flee the country at rates of over four hundred a week . . . We have reports also that hundreds of Namibian workers have been sacked from their jobs for having met with the UN fact-finding mission which visited Namibia in September this year".[7]

126

In a report published on 28 November 1978, a week before polling was due to begin, the ecumenical Christian Centre in Windhoek detailed a long list of alleged irregularities in voter registration, collected from witnesses throughout the country.[8] The Report stated that when registration began at the end of June, people were told over the South African-controlled radio that they had to register if they wanted to vote in UN-controlled elections. Many did so in this belief, but were later disillusioned when they heard Pastor Ndjoba, Chief Minister of the Ovambo bantustan and one of the DTA leaders, claim that the initial high registration rate was evidence of the trust people had in his tribal government and in the DTA. When the registration rate fell off, the provisions of Justice Steyn's *Proclamation AG* 37 were brought into effect. The election regulations set out in AG 37 made it an offence to dissuade, intimidate or prevent anyone from registering, but it did not make it an offence to use such means to *achieve* registration. In other words, those who contemplated using coercion against SWAPO supporters were given a *carte blanche*.

Intimidation was used constantly and blatantly throughout the registration campaign by the bantustan leaders, the South African administration, army and police, and white employers, according to the Report. One of the Ovambo ministers, Akwenya Shikongo, threatened people in Olutenyi on 7 July that "something will happen to you if you do not register". On 8 October he said over Radio Ovambo: "There is no place for you if you do not register and vote". Similar messages went out through other chiefs and headmen.

Teachers and nurses were told that they would be dismissed and punished as SWAPO supporters, if they did not vote. Patients were similarly intimidated. For instance, at Okahao Hospital, nurses were surprised when people coming for medical attention started to produce their registration cards; they had been told they would get no treatment without these documents. On 18 September workers at Oshakati Post Office were shown a cable stating that all Post Office employees must register. A Lutheran pastor found that pensioners were queuing up at the Okahandja Post Office with their registration cards because they had been told that their pensions would not be paid without this proof. On 4 July pension officials arrived at Onawa together with a registration team and army escort; pensioners who refused to register were turned away without their pensions.

There were many documented incidents of army and police roadblocks checking on registration cards. For instance, on 14 November, south of Engela, "soldiers travelling with four armoured cars asked travellers, shopowners and shoppers for their registration cards. One man from a nearby house was forced at gunpoint to fetch his card". On the same day a priest and a teacher who did not have cards were taken by a Lieutenant Visagie to a senior officer, who subsequently released them. Throughout this period soldiers were seen to greet people with the DTA sign.

The Report also confirmed allegations made previously by SWAPO, that substantial numbers of people who were not eligible had been registered, including children, Angolan refugees and South African whites without the requisite four year residential qualifications. The churches estimated that in the Kavango bantustan, more than a third of all people registered came from Angola.

In the urban areas and white farming zones, the Christian Centre reported that "present indications are that employers, in both the public and private sectors, played a crucial role in getting black people to register". Farmers' associations and other employers' interest groups may also have been involved. A worker in Walvis Bay, for example, gave the following statement:

On the 11 of September 1978 my boss approached me and asked which party I belonged to. I answered evasively. It then emerged that he is a staunch DTA supporter. The next morning my boss insisted that I must register. I made it clear that I did not want to register, saying that I was born in Walvis Bay. (*Note: Walvis Bay is claimed by the South African government as part of South Africa, and was in fact annexed into Cape Province in 1977. People born in Walvis Bay were not in theory permitted to register for the elections, unless they had lived for four years in Namibia outside of Walvis Bay*).

I insisted that I would bring him my birth certificate so that he could see for himself. The next morning I pretended that I had forgotten my birth certificate at home, as I was actually born in Windhoek. When the truth emerged he said that I should go to the registration office in Swakopmund and register. I said I was not interested in registering. He then sent me home and said that I should report the next day and tell him whether I had registered and wanted to stay or whether I wanted to leave his services. As I have three dependents I decided to register, but now I fear that the same thing will happen when the elections come.[9]

Unemployment among black Namibians continued to run at a high level at the end of 1978; the loss of one's job was a particularly threatening prospect. In a statement issued in Windhoek a fortnight before polling was due to begin SWAPO estimated that a total of 120,000 black workers had been coerced or blackmailed into registering by the threat of losing their jobs and or salaries. Out of the total eligible population, no more than 30% had registered voluntarily, SWAPO concluded, and these often out of ignorance.[10]

## Voting procedure

During polling itself, from 4-8 December 1978, similar allegations of widespread irregularities and intimidation were made by SWAPO and the mainstream of the church, and by a number of other political parties. Military vehicles and aircraft were used to collect voters from their homes and transport them to the polling booths. Here, they were expected to vote under the close supervision of armed police, South African troops, and armed officials of the Democratic Turnhalle Alliance. In addition to the regular polling stations, over 100 "mobile polling booths" were established under regulations enacted by Justice Steyn. These were mounted on the back of government vehicles and were accompanied by military and police escorts. Whereas the conventional polling stations were open from 7 a.m. to 7 p.m., the mobile booths were authorized to enter land or other private property at any time of the day or night, to find out whether anyone was present who was not registered or who had not voted, and to collect their vote there and then. Black Namibians, confronted in this way by the South African establishment, would have had no option but to cast their vote.[11]

The pressure to vote also came through the workplace. DTA members armed with automatic weapons patrolled the contract workers' hostel in Katutura. White employers collected up their black workers and made sure they got to the polling booths. Around Swakopmund, it was reported that railway workers who showed reluctance to vote had been threatened by the police.[12] Other sources reported that in several mining companies, workers who failed to vote for the DTA were threatened with dismissal. People in the liaison committee structure set up by a number of companies as an alternative to trade union organization were encouraged to do pro-DTA work.[13] SWAPO's acting Publicity and Information Secretary inside Namibia, Mr. Philip Tjerije, subsequently issued a list of major firms in the territory which had forced their black workers to vote.[14]

The experience of black workers employed by Consolidated Diamond Mines at Oranjemund, on the other hand, illustrated what the results of the election campaign might have been throughout Namibia, had conditions of genuine freedom existed. The parent company, De Beers, has followed a policy of permitting SWAPO members to operate openly at the Oranjemund mine, and SWAPO meetings have been held in the black workers' compounds (*see Ch. V*). CDM's black workforce is reputedly better organised than elsewhere in Namibia. At Oranjemund there was an almost total boycott of the registration process—only 6% of the 5,200 black workers employed by CDM were reported to have registered to vote, compared with 40—50% of the white staff. According to the mine's Public Relations Officer, this could be attributed to the fact that most of CDM's black employees were migrant workers from Ovamboland who supported SWAPO. CDM had a neutral political approach to the elections, he said. The company did nothing to persuade or dissuade its employees either way, but allowed them to hold meetings and to distribute posters and literature either for or against the elections.[15]

**Strike action**

It seems that the overtly pro-South African stance adopted by many white employers during the December elections may have been one of the factors which later prompted large scale strike action by black workers at a number of mines in Namibia.[16] The Rössing Uranium mine near Swakopmund, in particular, experienced the most serious industrial dispute in its history.

Strike action was first reported at Rössing on Friday 22 December 1978, when about 2,000 of the 3,000 African and Coloured workers employed at the mine stopped work. According to a spokesman for the mine management, the dispute had arisen over the planned introduction of new wage rates, based on the internationally-recognised Patterson job evaluation system. The Rössing management maintained that the Patterson system would eliminate racial discrimination at the mine by placing both black and white workers on the same wage curve. Most employees, furthermore, stood to gain increases of between 10 and 20% from the beginning of 1979.[17]

In a statement issued by Pastor Festus Naholo, SWAPO's National Secretary for Foreign Relations, however, SWAPO pointed out that while these increases meant that black workers would earn an additional R8 per month, the lowest paid white workers would receive an extra R100-200 per month. In other words, racial discrepancies would remain, even if the old division into those paid on the day rate system (i.e. the vast majority of black workers) and the staff rate system (including all whites) was abolished. This discovery had caused "widespread dissatisfaction" among the black workforce. (According to information supplied by RTZ in 1978, 1,821 out of a total of 2,163 hourly paid employees at Rössing were paid R230 a month or less at that time, while 717 out of a total of 835 monthly salaried staff received at least R440 a month, rising to more than R1,400).[18]

Pastor Naholo, whose church ministry covers the Arandis township developed by Rössing Uranium to accommodate its black employees, stated that there was a number of other grievances:

● there was no protection from the poisonous effects of uranium radiation
● the South African security police were responsible for bad treatment at the mine
● the health and welfare of black workers were granted low priority and there was a lack of recreational facilities
● black workers were accommodated in unsanitary single men's quarters while whites secured good housing in Swakopmund at nominal rent
● Rössing's black employees had been prevented from getting their side of the story across to overseas journalists who had been brought to the mine as part of a public relations exercise.

In conclusion, SWAPO reaffirmed its opposition to multinational companies operating illegally in Namibia, in defiance of Decree No. 1 of the United Nations Council for Namibia for the protection of the territory's natural resources.[19]

On 28 December the striking workers were reported to be back at work, but negotiations were continuing with the Rössing management. A committee was subsequently reported to have been established to investigate their grievances.[20] According to a spokesman for the strikers, the miners had gone back to work once their request for a minimum wage of R175 a month had been granted.[21]

Over the next few days, at least three other mines were reported to be affected by industrial disputes. At the Kranzberg wolfram mine near Omaruru, owned

130

by Noord Mining, 208 out of 270 black miners were sacked from their jobs after going on strike on 2 January to demand a wage increase. The 208 miners were put on a train to Ovamboland that same evening and replacements sought. At the Uis tin mine, owned by the SA Iron and Steel Corporation (ISCOR), about 500 Ovambo and Damara workers went on a three day strike. At the Tsumeb copper mine, jointly owned by two US companies, mineworkers were also reported to be making pay demands, though a strike did not develop.[22] On 5 January, the Managing Director of Tsumeb Corporation Ltd., Mr. G. R. Parker, said that wage increments had been paid to the approximately 4,000 employees of the mine. "The uneasiness and unrest among mine workers" elsewhere in Namibia had, he said, "necessitated an adjustment". He did not reveal the size of the wage rises.[23]

According to the *Windhoek Advertiser*, spokesmen for the workers had been demanding pay increases of more than 300% from between R2.60—R2.80 a shift to R8—R20 a shift. (Normally there is one shift per day). This had been rejected by the mine management, which had previously announced that the annual bonus for all workers would be eliminated and replaced by an immediate 5% increase in wages. The newspaper also revealed that the South African police had been called in to raid the Tsumeb compounds when the strike threatened, and had evicted over 500 people alleged to be living there illegally.[24]

In Swakopmund, Pastor Festus Naholo and four other SWAPO members connected with Rössing were arrested and detained under the Terrorism Act.[25] The arrests took place shortly after a bomb had exploded in a Swakopmund bakery on 30 December—an incident which the police seem to have used as a pretext for removing from the scene those suspected of playing a leading role in the Rössing dispute. According to the *Windhoek Advertiser*, the police had discovered "a possible link" between the "SWAPO—inspired strike" at Rössing and the Swakopmund bomb explosion. No details or further evidence of any such link was reported by the newspaper, beyond a statement that it was "understood" that a number of senior officials at Rössing had allegedly received "threatening calls" from SWAPO members shortly before the bomb blast.[26]

According to the London *Financial Times*, "observers in Windhoek believe that the strike may have been political, as a protest against the recent elections".[27]

# Appendix B — References

1. *FOCUS* 17, July 1978, p. 9.
2. *WA* 19, June 1978.
3. *FOCUS* 17, July 1978, p. 9.
4. *FOCUS* 20, January—February 1979, p. 16
5. *WO* 28 October 1978.
6. *WO* 18 November 1978.
7. SWAPO Press Release, London, 2 November 1978.
8. *Report on the Registration and Election Campaign in Namibia*, 1978, published by the Christian Centre in Namibia, 28 November 1978. Mr. Justin Ellis, the acting Director of the Christian Centre who was responsible for the compilation of the report, was deported from Namibia a week before polling was due to begin.
9. ibid.
10. Statement issued in Windhoek, 23 November 1978.
11. *FOCUS* 20, January—February 1979, p. 2.
12. *De Groene Amsterdammer* 20 December 1978; *Obs.* 10 December 1978.
13. *Report from a visitor to Namibia: December 1978*, published by the Namibia Support Committee, London.
14. *WO* 22 December 1978.
15. *WA* 5 December 1978.
16. During the build-up to the elections, there were somewhat conflicting reports that SWAPO was calling for a general strike to coincide with five days of voting. It was in response to these that the South African authorities announced at the end of November that from now on they would treat strikers as criminals (*see Ch. IX*). SWAPO officials inside Namibia, however, stated that it was not their intention to call a general strike, as this would simply provide the South African authorities with a pretext to clamp down upon SWAPO members through arrest and detention. They were however calling for a boycott of the election process, even if this meant confrontation with employers. (*RDM* 21 November 1978, SWAPO statement issued in Windhoek, 23 November 1978).
17. *WA* 27 December 1978.
18. RTZ *Fact Sheet No. 2*, 18 May 1978; *see also Ch. V.*
19. SWAPO Press Statement, issued in Windhoek, 22 December 1978.
20. *WA* 28 December 1978; *RDM* 29 December 1978, *FT* 9 January 1979.
21. *WO* 13 January 1979.
22. *WA* 3 January 1979, *FT* 5 January 1979.
23. *WO* 6 January 1979.
24. *WA* 9 January 1979.
25. The others detained were all employees of Rössing: Mr. Arthur Pickering (who was the first Coloured advocate to be admitted to the bar in Namibia); Mr. Henry Boonzaaier; Mr. Ombadja Oshuna and Mr. Philippus Namuleme. The last two were both described as Ovambo-speaking residents of Arandis township. (*WO* 6 January 1979).
26. *WA* 2 January 1979.
27. *FT* 29 December 1978.

# Index

133

134

# A Selected List of
# IDAF PUBLICATIONS

### A DWELLING PLACE OF OUR OWN    40p
#### (rev. ed. 1975, 52pp illustrated)
The Story of the Namibian Nation by Randolph Vigne
"This is a committed account."  Times Literary Supplement.

### PRISONERS OF APARTHEID    £3.00
#### (1978, 180pp)
A biographical list of political prisoners and banned persons in
South Africa.  In addition the book contains a list of known
Namibian political prisoners held in South African prisons.

### ZIMBABWE: THE FACTS ABOUT RHODESIA    60p
#### (1977, 84pp illustrated)
"A well organised, copiously illustrated compendium of informa-
tion on the history and economic structure of white rule in
Rhodesia."  In These Times (Chicago).

### SMITH'S SETTLEMENT    50p
#### (1978, 37pp)
Events in Zimbabwe since 3rd March 1978.
Shows that there is no genuine commitment on the part of Ian
Smith to hand over power to the majority of the people.

### THIS IS APARTHEID    20p
#### (1978, 36pp illustrated)
"Contains more than 50 photographs which capture the brutality
of apartheid more than any other publication." – Tribune.

### NELSON MANDELA - THE STRUGGLE IS MY LIFE £1.85
#### (1979, 210pp illustrated)
A major collection of Mandela's speeches and writings.

*Available from*
*IDAF Publications* 104 *Newgate Street, London EC1A 7AP*

*Printed by* A. G. Bishop & Sons Ltd., Orpington, Kent.